United States Nuclear Regulatory Commission

Protecting People and the Environment

NUREG-2119

Mechanical Behavior of Ballooned and Ruptured Cladding

Office of Nuclear Regulatory Research

AVAILABILITY OF REFERENCE MATERIALS
IN NRC PUBLICATIONS

NRC Reference Material

As of November 1999, you may electronically access NUREG-series publications and other NRC records at NRC's Public Electronic Reading Room at http://www.nrc.gov/reading-rm.html.
Publicly released records include, to name a few, NUREG-series publications; *Federal Register* notices; applicant, licensee, and vendor documents and correspondence; NRC correspondence and internal memoranda; bulletins and information notices; inspection and investigative reports; licensee event reports; and Commission papers and their attachments.

NRC publications in the NUREG series, NRC regulations, and *Title 10, Energy*, in the Code of *Federal Regulations* may also be purchased from one of these two sources.
1. The Superintendent of Documents
    U.S. Government Printing Office
    Mail Stop SSOP
    Washington, DC 20402–0001
    Internet: bookstore.gpo.gov
    Telephone: 202-512-1800
    Fax: 202-512-2250
2. The National Technical Information Service
    Springfield, VA 22161–0002
    www.ntis.gov
    1–800–553–6847 or, locally, 703–605–6000

A single copy of each NRC draft report for comment is available free, to the extent of supply, upon written request as follows:
Address: U.S. Nuclear Regulatory Commission
            Office of Administration
            Publications Branch
            Washington, DC 20555-0001
E-mail: DISTRIBUTION.SERVICES@NRC.GOV
Facsimile: 301–415–2289

Some publications in the NUREG series that are posted at NRC's Web site address http://www.nrc.gov/reading-rm/doc-collections/nuregs are updated periodically and may differ from the last printed version. Although references to material found on a Web site bear the date the material was accessed, the material available on the date cited may subsequently be removed from the site.

Non-NRC Reference Material

Documents available from public and special technical libraries include all open literature items, such as books, journal articles, and transactions, *Federal Register* notices, Federal and State legislation, and congressional reports. Such documents as theses, dissertations, foreign reports and translations, and non-NRC conference proceedings may be purchased from their sponsoring organization.

Copies of industry codes and standards used in a substantive manner in the NRC regulatory process are maintained at—
    The NRC Technical Library
    Two White Flint North
    11545 Rockville Pike
    Rockville, MD 20852–2738

These standards are available in the library for reference use by the public. Codes and standards are usually copyrighted and may be purchased from the originating organization or, if they are American National Standards, from—
    American National Standards Institute
    11 West 42nd Street
    New York, NY 10036–8002
    www.ansi.org
    212–642–4900

Legally binding regulatory requirements are stated only in laws; NRC regulations; licenses, including technical specifications; or orders, not in NUREG-series publications. The views expressed in contractor-prepared publications in this series are not necessarily those of the NRC.

The NUREG series comprises (1) technical and administrative reports and books prepared by the staff (NUREG–XXXX) or agency contractors (NUREG/CR–XXXX), (2) proceedings of conferences (NUREG/CP–XXXX), (3) reports resulting from international agreements (NUREG/IA–XXXX), (4) brochures (NUREG/BR–XXXX), and (5) compilations of legal decisions and orders of the Commission and Atomic and Safety Licensing Boards and of Directors' decisions under Section 2.206 of NRC's regulations (NUREG–0750).

United States Nuclear Regulatory Commission

Protecting People and the Environment

NUREG-2119

Mechanical Behavior of Ballooned and Ruptured Cladding

Manuscript Completed: February 2012
Date Published: February 2012

Prepared by
Michelle Flanagan

Office of Nuclear Regulatory Research

ABSTRACT

This report presents and discusses the results of the NRC's integral loss-of-coolant accident (LOCA) research program. In this program, the residual bending moment and failure energy were measured using the four point bend tests for as-received and irradiated samples following exposure to LOCA conditions to determine the resistance to fracturing of ballooned cladding. The findings of this research program have been used to develop a recommendation for how to treat the ballooned region in LOCA analysis. To support the recommendation, this document will begin with a review of the regulatory history of the balloon region, present a discussion of available test methods for measuring post-LOCA cladding behavior, present the results of bend tests on as-fabricated and irradiated cladding material following exposure to LOCA conditions, and conclude with recommendations for using this information to inform regulatory decisions. The purpose of this document is to serve as the technical basis for the treatment of the ballooned and ruptured regions of a fuel rod in LOCA analysis.

FOREWORD

The purpose of this document is to serve as the technical basis for the treatment of the ballooned and ruptured regions of a fuel rod in loss-of-coolant accident (LOCA) analysis. The technical basis is founded on the results of the NRC's integral LOCA research program, which was designed to measure the mechanical behavior of ballooned and ruptured cladding following LOCA conditions. Integral LOCA tests were conducted at Argonne National Laboratory and Studsvik Laboratory in Sweden. The results and observations of the two experimental programs have been combined to develop conclusions about the impact of oxidation, hydrogen content and burnup on the mechanical behavior of ballooned and ruptured cladding following LOCA conditions. These conclusions have been used to develop a recommendation for the treatment of the ballooned and ruptured regions of a fuel rod in LOCA analysis.

The recommendation for the treatment of ballooned and ruptured regions of a fuel rod in LOCA analysis is to limit oxidation by the time-at-temperature limit developed based on ring-compression data, with the provisions for the balloon outlined in the existing rule to use the average wall thickness in the rupture region to calculate the equivalent cladding reacted (ECR).

TABLE OF CONTENTS

TABLE OF FIGURES

LIST OF TABLES

ABBREVIATIONS AND ACRONYMS

4-PBT – Four-point bend test

ANL – Argonne National Laboratory

CP-ECR – Equivalent Cladding Reacted as calculated by the Cathcart-Pawel Oxidation equation

ECR – Equivalent Cladding Reacted

JAEA – Japan Atomic Energy Agency

LOCA – Loss-of-Coolant Accident

RCT – Ring Compression Test

1. PURPOSE AND INTRODUCTION

The purpose of this document is to serve as the technical basis for the treatment of the ballooned and ruptured regions of a fuel rod in loss-of-coolant accident (LOCA) analysis.

In the United States, the LOCA acceptance criteria implemented in 1973 in Title 10 of the *Code of Federal Regulations* (10 CFR) 50.46(b) (Ref. 1) limit the peak cladding temperature to 2,200 degrees Fahrenheit (F) and the maximum oxidation level to 17 percent of the cladding wall thickness, assuming that all of the oxygen picked up by the cladding is in the form of zirconium oxide (ZrO_2). These criteria are intended to assure that cladding retains some ductility during and following quench. According to the Atomic Energy Commission in 1973, "Our selection of the 2200°F limit results primarily from our belief that retention of ductility in the zircaloy is the best guarantee of its remaining intact during the hypothetical LOCA" (Ref. 2).

The LOCA acceptance criteria implemented in 1973 were based largely on ring-compression tests (RCTs) to assess the oxidation and temperature limits at which embrittlement occurs. The data available at the time were largely from as-fabricated and low-burnup cladding materials. In July 1998, the U.S. Nuclear Regulatory Commission (NRC) adopted a research plan to investigate the effects of operation to high burnup on LOCAs and other events. Like the program that defined the LOCA acceptance criteria implemented in 1973, this test program used RCTs to assess the oxidation and temperature limits at which embrittlement occurs. Staying close to the existing basis and emergency core cooling system computations was an important regulatory consideration. The effects on cladding embrittlement of both alloy composition and burnup were studied in this research program. The results of this research revealed that the cladding corrosion, which occurs as fuel burnup increases, has a substantial effect on embrittlement. The results of the program also indicated that, if the cladding corrosion was considered in terms of absorbed hydrogen, the embrittlement behavior of all zirconium-alloy cladding materials tested could be characterized by a common trend.

The Office of Nuclear Regulatory Research issued Research Information Letter (RIL)-0801, "Technical Basis for Revision of Embrittlement Criteria in 10 CFR 50.46," in May 2008 (Ref. 3), recommending that the experimental results from the NRC's LOCA research program be considered as the basis for rulemaking. An interoffice working group was formed to support rulemaking revisions.

The majority of the cladding embrittlement experimental results from the NRC's LOCA research program are summarized in NUREG/CR-6967, "Cladding Embrittlement during Postulated Loss-of-Coolant Accidents," issued July 2008 (Ref. 4). Since the publication of NUREG/CR-6967 and RIL-0801 in 2008, additional testing has been conducted, focusing on cladding materials with hydrogen contents in the 200 to 350 weight parts per million (wppm) range (Refs. 5-6). When the tests that were conducted after the publication of NUREG/CR-6967 were combined with the data reported in NUREG/CR-6967, the resulting behavior description of cladding embrittlement as a function of hydrogen content could be depicted as shown in Figure 1. The data points and trend lines mark the transition from ductile to brittle behavior, as observed in RCTs, of oxidized as-fabricated, prehydrided, and high-burnup cladding materials.

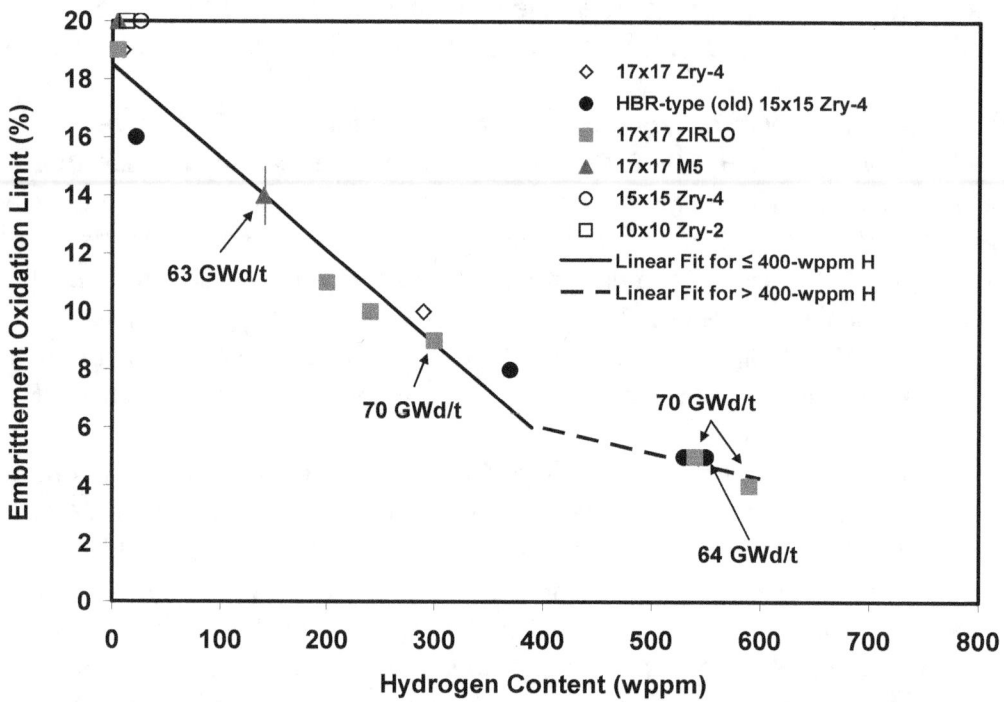

Figure 1 **Embrittlement oxidation limit (CP-ECR in %) as a function of metal hydrogen content for as-fabricated, prehydrided, and high-burnup cladding alloys oxidized at a peak temperature of 1,200 °C, quenched at 800 °C, and ring-compressed at 135 °C. Oxidation values above data points and trend lines resulted in brittle behavior. For hydrogen contents in the range of 540–600 wppm, peak cladding temperatures (1,130–1,180 °C) occurred during the heating ramp at <1,200 °C (Ref. 6).**

In developing rule language for a revision to 10 CFR 50.46(b), the staff discussion focused on how to treat the portion of the fuel rod predicted to balloon and rupture during a LOCA. In particular, the staff discussed whether the hydrogen-based embrittlement correlation derived from RCTs, shown above in Figure 1, was the appropriate limit to apply in the balloon region. Discussion of complications associated with applying the ductility-based criteria to the ballooned region is not apparent in the historical record of the rule implemented in 1973. RIL-0801 states that "no criteria have been found that would ensure ductility in the cladding balloon. However, loss of ductility in this short portion of a fuel rod should not lead to an uncoolable geometry as long as the amount of oxidation in the ballooned region remains limited in the current manner" (Ref. 3). The staff discussion within the working group focused on how to document and support this statement in the rulemaking Statements of Consideration.

In an effort to resolve the staff discussion about the treatment of the balloon region, the working group staff turned to the results coming out of the NRC's integral LOCA research program. The integral LOCA research program was designed to measure the mechanical behavior of ballooned and ruptured cladding following LOCA conditions.[1] In this program, four-point-bend tests (4-PBTs) were being used to determine post-LOCA sample failure location, maximum bending moment (measure of strength), failure energy (measure of toughness), and offset displacement (measure of plastic displacement).

In the NRC's integral LOCA research program, residual bending moment and failure energy were measured using the 4-PBT for as-received and irradiated samples following exposure to LOCA conditions to determine the resistance to fracturing of ballooned. The findings of this research program have been used to develop a recommendation for how to treat the ballooned region within the rulemaking to revise 10 CFR 50.46(b). To support this recommendation, this document will begin with a review of the regulatory history of the balloon region, present a discussion of available test methods for measuring post-LOCA cladding behavior, present the results of bend tests on as-fabricated and irradiated cladding material following exposure to LOCA conditions, and conclude with recommendations for using this information to inform regulatory decisions.

2. REGULATORY HISTORY OF THE BALLOON REGION

There have been multiple thoughtful and thorough reviews of the history of LOCA embrittlement criteria, and there are many excellent resources documenting the development of the embrittlement criteria (Refs. 7-8). The full history of LOCA embrittlement criteria will not be documented here, and the reader is encouraged to review the abovementioned references for more complete background. The intention of the brief historical summary provided in this section is to provide context for the remainder of the report.

The LOCA rule adopted in 1973 included acceptance criteria for peak cladding temperature (2,200 degrees F) and maximum cladding oxidation (17 percent). In its final opinion statement, the Atomic Energy Commission said that "the purpose of these first two criteria is to ensure that...the cladding would remain in one piece if it were not too heavily oxidized, and would still restrain the UO_2 pellets" (Ref. 2). The testimony in the rulemaking hearing relied considerably on the demonstrated survival of specimens in quench tests. Arguments based on strength and loads arguments were made. In summary, however, the Atomic Energy Commission stated that "retention of ductility in the zircaloy is the best guarantee of its remaining intact during the hypothetical LOCA" (Ref. 2).

Although it was not discussed in the Commission's opinion statement, retention of ductility in the cladding has inherent benefits. In the absence of a credible analysis of loads, cladding stresses, and cladding strains for a degraded LOCA core, there are no absolute metrics to determine how much ductility or strength would be needed to "guarantee" that fuel-rod cladding would maintain its geometry during and following LOCA quench. It is also not clear what impact the severing of some fuel rods into two pieces would have on core coolability. Even minimal ductility ensures that cladding will have high strength and toughness and therefore high

---

[1]   See Appendix A for a discussion of the test train and experimental design used to induce LOCA conditions and the comparison to postulated in-reactor LOCA conditions.

resistance to fracturing. Fully brittle cladding, on the other hand, might fail at low strength and shatter. Therefore, the intent to maintain ductility is beneficial even without adequate knowledge of LOCA loads.

The LOCA acceptance criteria implemented in 1973 provided the following guidance for the application of the ductility-based oxidation criteria in ballooned and ruptured regions (see 10 CFR 50.46(b) (Ref. 1)):

> If cladding rupture is calculated to occur, the inside surfaces of the cladding shall be included in the oxidation, beginning at the calculated time of rupture. Cladding thickness before oxidation means the radial distance from inside to outside the cladding, after any calculated rupture or swelling has occurred but before significant oxidation. Where the calculated conditions of transient pressure and temperature lead to a prediction of cladding swelling, with or without cladding rupture, the unoxidized cladding thickness shall be defined as the cladding cross-sectional area, taken at a horizontal plane at the elevation of the rupture, if it occurs, or at the elevation of the highest cladding temperature if no rupture is calculated to occur, divided by the average circumference at that elevation. For ruptured cladding the circumference does not include the rupture opening.

Discussion of complications associated with applying the ductility-based oxidation criteria to the ballooned region is not apparent in the historical record. Complications in the balloon arise from several sources. The first is the cladding wall in the ballooned region, which is neither contiguous nor of constant thickness. This is illustrated in the cross section shown in Figure 2 with the rupture opening at the bottom of the figure. It is apparent that some of the cladding near the rupture opening is very thin and will in all likelihood be brittle even though the material opposite the rupture may be ductile. Recognition of this fact by the 1973 Atomic Energy Commission—that ductility is not maintained circumferentially in the balloon—can be assumed because the rule language quoted above specifies a method of using average wall thickness for oxidation calculations.

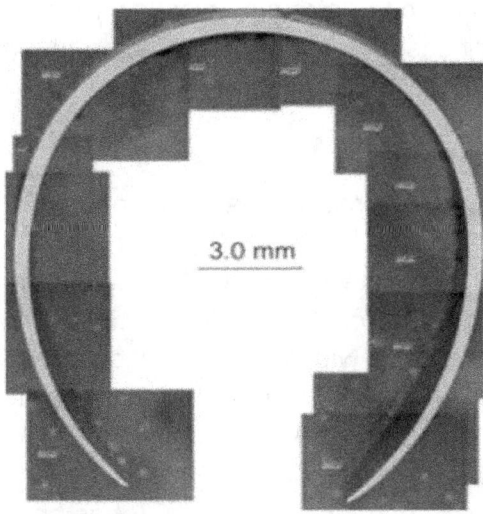

Figure 2 Ballooned and ruptured ZIRLO cladding (ANL)

A second complication was discovered after the rulemaking was completed. Research reported in the early 1980s in both the United States (NRC) and Japan (Japan Atomic Energy Research Institute) found regions of high hydrogen concentration just above and below the rupture location. This was a consequence of oxidation of the inside cladding surface by steam, which enters through the rupture opening. Research in both countries found that these neck regions in the balloon could be brittle. As a consequence, there are several regions in a balloon in which ductility may not be maintained even if the acceptance criteria in 10 CFR 50.46, "Acceptance Criteria for Emergency Core Cooling Systems for Light-Water Nuclear Power Reactors," are satisfied.

Nevertheless, the U.S. and Japanese researchers in 1980 concluded that the oxidation limits in 10 CFR 50.46(b) (Ref. 1) were conservative based on two findings: (1) ballooned specimens survived quenching with very high oxidation levels, and (2) quenched specimens did not fracture when modest loads were applied as long as the calculated oxidation level was less than the regulatory limit, calculated as defined by the LOCA acceptance criteria implemented in 1973. With these findings in hand, the NRC made no change in the LOCA acceptance criteria.

3. DISCUSSION OF AVAILABLE TEST METHODS FOR MEASURING POST-LOCA BEHAVIOR

Several types of tests have been used within the nuclear community to characterize cladding mechanical behavior following LOCA conditions. Each test provides advantages and disadvantages and is useful for developing various conclusions. Two test methods are being used predominantly as ductility screening tests for nondeformed cladding after exposure to LOCA oxidation and quench: RCTs and three-point bend tests (3-PBTs). Two test methods are being used predominantly to assess the performance of ballooned and ruptured cladding following oxidation: postquench 4-PBTs and partial-to-full axial restraint tests during quench.

5

Other test methods have been used to determine plastic stress-strain behavior and ductility for cladding materials under conditions relevant to normal operation and reactivity initiated accidents such as axial tensile tests, hoop tensile tests, and tests with combined axial and hoop tensile stresses.

These test methods are described in Argonne National Laboratory's (ANL's) letter report, "Test Methods for Post-LOCA Cladding," dated March 15, 2011 (Ref. 9). The report discusses each test method and summarizes their relative advantages and disadvantages for determining cladding performance following LOCA oxidation. An expanded version of this letter report will be published in 2012 as a NUREG/CR with the title, "Assessment of Current Test Methods for Post-LOCA Cladding Behavior." A full discussion of available test methods will not be documented here; the reader is encouraged to review the letter report (Ref. 9) for more complete background. In addition to the reports written by ANL, the subject of test methods to measure cladding behavior during and following a LOCA has been addressed in a number of other reports. One such report was written in 2007 by the Special Expert Group on Fuel Safety Margins assembled by the Nuclear Energy Agency's (NEA) Committee on the Safety of Nuclear Installations (CSNI) titled, "LOCA Fuel Cladding Test Methodologies, Compilation of Responses and Recommended Test Characteristics Technical Note" (Ref. 10). This report aimed to collect and analyze information on current LOCA tests and evaluation methodologies and discuss their advantages and disadvantages. Another report titled, "Review of High Burn-up RIA and LOCA Database and Criteria" (Ref. 11) also discusses LOCA experiments. This document was intended to provide regulators, their technical support organizations and industry with a concise review of existing fuel experimental data at RIA and LOCA conditions and considerations on how these data affect fuel safety criteria at increasing burn-up. Finally, a report on the subject of LOCA test methods was issued in 2011 by the NEA/CSNI Working Group on Fuel Safety and titled, "Technical Opinion Paper on LOCA Criteria Basis and Test Methodology" (Ref. 12). The purpose of this report was to review the LOCA criteria basis and the different test methodologies used to support the basis, and to provide recommendations to the international community on how the results of these different methodologies can be applied for regulatory purposes.

The intention of the brief summary provided in this section is to provide background on available test methods.

3.1 Ductility Screening Tests

The nuclear community is predominantly using two test methods as ductility screening tests for nondeformed cladding after exposure to LOCA oxidation and quench: RCTs and 3-PBTs.

The LOCA acceptance criteria implemented in 1973 in the United States were based on RCTs to assess the oxidation and temperature limits at which embrittlement occurs. Ring-compression loading induces circumferential bending stresses in post-LOCA cladding samples. Under the load and above the support, the hoop stresses across the cladding wall vary from maximum tensile stress (inner surface) to maximum compressive (outer surface). At ±90° from the loading direction, the hoop stress distribution is reversed (i.e., compressive inner- and tensile outer-surface hoop stresses). Ring-compression loading is not considered prototypical of anticipated loads on the cladding during quench, including axial stresses due to bending, axial stresses due to restricted thermal contraction of the cladding, and possible impact loading in the balloon region.

Three-point bend tests are another method of measuring ductility. The 3-PBT has an advantage over the RCT because loading and unloading stiffness values in bend tests should be essentially the same, and therefore interpretation of load-displacement curves is more straightforward. In addition, because axial stresses are likely to occur during LOCA quench, the 3-PBT loading, which induces axial tensile stresses on the convex surface of the bent sample, is more LOCA-relevant. However, it can be inferred from data produced internationally that no significant difference exists between embrittlement oxidation levels determined from ring tests (hoop bending stress) and axial bend tests (axial bending stress). The results of testing conducted at Commissariate à l'Energie Atomique laboratory in France indicate that, if the prior-beta layer is brittle in the hoop direction, it will also be brittle in the axial direction (Refs. 13-14).

With these considerations, the 3-PBT is the best choice for post-LOCA embrittlement determination of nondeformed as-fabricated and prehydrided samples that are uniformly oxidized. Under the same conditions, the RCT is preferred for irradiated samples because these tests require far less material. However, it is desirable to have a single test method for as-fabricated, prehydrided, and irradiated cladding to eliminate systematic errors when comparing the behavior of these materials. For such a study, the RCT is preferred.

3.2 Assessing the Performance of Ballooned and Ruptured Cladding

There are three locations of interest in assessing the performance of ballooned and ruptured cladding following exposure to LOCA conditions: the rupture location (where the average wall thickness is the thinnest making the oxidation percentage the highest), and two locations on either side of the rupture location (where the high hydrogen content is found coincident with intermediate oxidation levels). Test methods used to assess the performance of ballooned and ruptured cladding must consider these three locations of interest.

RCTs with samples sectioned from the balloon region are not appropriate tests because of the steep variation in outer diameter. Loading would be highly localized at the point of maximum outer diameter, and it would spread axially as the cladding deformed or cracked. Three-point bend tests would also not be appropriate for measuring the performance of ballooned and ruptured cladding because they bias the failure location to coincide with the loading location. The nuclear community is predominantly using two test methods to assess the performance of ballooned and ruptured cladding following oxidation: postquench 4-PBTs and partial-to-full axial restraint tests during quench.

The 4-PBT can be used to assess the performance of ballooned and ruptured cladding following oxidation and to determine post-LOCA sample failure location (among the three locations of interest in and around the rupture region), maximum bending moment (measure of strength), failure energy (measure of toughness), and offset displacement (measure of plastic displacement).

Partial-to-full axial restraint tests during quench can also be used to assess the performance of ballooned and ruptured cladding following oxidation. Pulling the sample to failure can be used to determine the sample failure location and would give an accurate measure of failure load. However, if the load displacement curve exhibited any offset displacement, it would not be clear if plastic displacement had occurred within the ballooned and ruptured region, just above and below this region where the temperature drops, or outside the middle region where the cladding is annealed and lightly oxidized with negligible hydrogen pickup. For samples that failed during quench, these tests generated data for failure load and location. For samples that did not fail during quench, no quantitative conclusions about the performance of the tested sample can be made other than to state that the failure strength must be larger than the applied load.

3.3 Test Method Chosen for the NRC LOCA Research Program To Assess the Performance of Ballooned and Ruptured Cladding

The objective of the NRC's LOCA research program was to assess the performance of ballooned and ruptured cladding and, specifically, to assess the impact of oxidation, hydrogen content, and burnup on the residual fuel rod mechanical behavior following LOCA conditions. With these objectives, the NRC chose the 4-PBT for the LOCA research program. The load displacement curve from the 4-PBT can be evaluated to generate quantitative information about the margin to failure of ballooned and ruptured cladding following LOCA conditions. The 4-PBT was used in testing at ANL and Studsvik to assess the performance of ballooned and ruptured cladding following oxidation and to determine post-LOCA sample failure location (relative to the three locations of interest in and around the rupture region), maximum bending moment (measure of strength), failure energy (measure of toughness), and offset displacement (measure of plastic displacement). As-fabricated cladding material was tested at ANL in 4-PBTs following LOCA conditions, and irradiated, high-burnup cladding material was tested at Studsvik in parallel experiments.

4. RESULTS AND DISCUSSION OF THE NRC'S LOCA RESEARCH PROGRAM TO ASSESS THE PERFORMANCE OF BALLOONED AND RUPTURED CLADDING

As-fabricated cladding material was tested at ANL in 4-PBTs following LOCA conditions, and irradiated, high-burnup cladding material was tested at Studsvik in parallel experiments. Four-point bend test results were used to determine post-LOCA sample failure location, maximum bending moment (measure of strength), failure energy (measure of toughness), and offset displacement (measure of plastic displacement) as a function of equivalent cladding reacted (ECR).

The bending moment (M) is determined from the applied lateral force in four-point loading. The maximum energy (E_{max}) is determined by calculating the area under the force versus displacement curve. The offset displacement is determined at the loading points. The four-point bend tests were conducted in the standard displacement-controlled mode at 1–

2 millimeters per second (mm/s) and a maximum displacement at the loading points of 14 millimeters (mm). In accordance with American Society for Testing and Materials standards for fracture toughness and Charpy impact tests, the load was applied to cladding at 180° relative to the rupture opening in order to subject the flawed rupture tips to maximum tensile stresses. Two tests were conducted at ANL on as-received cladding with the rupture tips subjected to maximum compressive stresses to determine the effects of sample orientation relative to the bending moment. This orientation is referred to as "reverse" bending in this report.

This section will discuss the results of the testing of as-fabricated cladding material and irradiated cladding material. Finally, comparison of the results as a function of ECR and between as-fabricated and irradiated material will be highlighted and discussed. In this report, when ECR values are reported for ballooned and ruptured cladding, the values have been determined using the Cathcart-Pawel Equation (CP-ECR), assuming double-sided oxidation and taking the average wall thickness in the rupture region in the calculation of the CP-ECR.

4.1 Results of Testing of As-Fabricated Cladding Material

Table 1 summarizes the ANL test conditions for ballooning, rupture, oxidation, and quench of pressurized, as-fabricated 17×17 ZIRLO™ LOCA integral samples.

Table 1 Test Conditions for Ballooning, Rupture, Oxidation, and Quench of Pressurized, As-Fabricated 17×17 ZIRLO LOCA Integral Samples.

Parameters	As-Fabricated
17×17 Cladding	ZIRLO
Clad OD, mm	9.5
Wall Thick., mm	0.57
Sample Length, mm (minus end caps)	295
Hydrogen Content, wppm	≈10
Pellets	zirconia
Pellet Stack Length, mm	280
Gas Volume, cm^3	10
Internal Pressure, MPa	4.1 to 8.3
(Gauge)	@300 °C
Heating Rate, °C/s	5
Rupture T, °C	843±6
	748±6
Rupture Strain, %	22±3
	45±4
Hold Temp., °C	1,200
Cooling Rate to Quench Temp., °C/s	3
Quench Temp., °C	800

Table 2 summarizes the 4-PBT results. All of the samples remained intact during quench. With the exception of the last test sample (OCZL#32) subjected to 4-PBT at room temperature, bending was conducted at 135 degrees Celsius (C) sample temperature. The table shows three metrics for assessing cladding performance: maximum bending moment, failure or maximum energy, and offset displacement. Also included in Table 2 are the failure locations relative to the center of the rupture opening. With the exception of the OCZL#25 sample, LOCA integral samples with circumferential strains less than or equal to 32 percent failed in a region where the cladding was fully brittle between the rupture tips and the hydrogen peaks. Samples with greater than or equal to 40 percent rupture strain failed in the rupture node location where some of the cladding had significant local ductility (e.g., thick back side of the balloon). None of the bend samples had rupture strains in the range of 33 to 39 percent. Results for the three metrics are discussed below.

Table 2 Summary of Results for LOCA Integral and Post-LOCA Bend Tests with As-Fabricated ZIRLO Cladding. OCZL refers to the "Out-of-Cell ZIRLO" test series. Reference LOCA Test Conditions Were 600- or 1,200-psig Fill Pressure at 300 °C, 5 °C/s Heating Rate to 1,200 °C, 1,200 °C Hold Temperature, 3 °C/s Cooling Rate to 800 °C, and Quench at 800 °C. Reference Conditions for 4-PBTs Were 135 °C Test Temperature and 2 mm/s Displacement Rate to 14-mm Maximum Displacement. The Displacement Rate Was Lowered to 1 mm/s after the OCZL#21 Bend Test.

Test ID OCZL#	Fill Pressure, psig	Rupture Strain, % (T_R, °C)	CP-ECR %	Quench at 800 °C	Stress in Rupture Node	Failure Location	Maximum Bending Moment N·m	Maximum Energy J	Offset Displace. mm
8	600	21 (845±25)	0	No	Maximum tension	No cracking	20.9	>8.4	>7.7
9	400	33 (875±15)	0	No	Maximum tension	No cracking	20.6	>8.3	>7.7
10	1,600	69 (715±10)	0	No	Maximum tension	No cracking	19.5	>7.7	>7.1
12	1,000	32 (805±20)	14	No	Maximum compression	-40 mm +33 mm	10.5	0.78	0
13	1,200	41 (741±15)	14	No	Maximum tension	Rupture opening	8.8	0.58	0
14	1,200	47 (735±6)	18	Yes	Maximum tension	Rupture opening	5.7	0.24	0
15	1,200	51 (755±23)	18	Yes	Maximum compression	Cracking; no failure	8.9	>2.3	>13
17	1,200	49 (750±17)	13	Yes	Maximum tension	Rupture opening	8.4	0.71	>0.5
18	1,200	43 (748±4)	12	Yes	Maximum tension	Rupture opening	13.5	1.29	0

Table 2. Summary of Results for LOCA Integral and Post-LOCA Bend Tests with As-Fabricated ZIRLO Cladding (Cont'd)

Test ID OCZL#	Fill Pressure, psig	Rupture Strain, % (T_R, °C)	CP-ECR %	Quench at 800 °C	Stress in Rupture Node	Failure Location	Maximum Bending Moment N·m	Maximum Energy J	Offset Displace. mm
19	600	24 (840±12)	17	Yes	Maximum tension	+23 mm -23 mm	5.7	0.23	0
21	600	27 (850±10)	10	Yes	Maximum tension	+33 mm -29 mm	13.8	1.17	0
22[a]	600	22 (837±12)	11	Yes	Maximum tension	+25 mm -27 mm	11.1	0.83	0
25[a]	1,200	42 (757±21)	16	Yes	Maximum tension	-26 mm +26 mm	8.3	0.50	0
29[a]	1,200	49 (746±19)	17	Yes	Maximum tension	Rupture opening	4.7	0.40	>8.5
32[a,b]	1,200	49 (748±8)	17	Yes	Maximum tension	Rupture opening	6.7	0.26	0

[a] Displacement rate lowered to 1 mm/s to get better agreement between bend and ring-compression tests for the maximum elastic strain rate.

[b] 4-PBT conducted at 30 °C.

4.1.1 Maximum Bending Moment

Three ramp-to-rupture samples with rupture strains ranging from 21 to 69 percent were subjected to 4-PBTs to determine reference values for maximum bending moment and energy at zero percent oxidation level (CP-ECR). After 14-mm displacement, the load-displacement curves were relatively flat, indicating that the end-of-test bending moments were close to their maximum values.

The maximum bending moment values for ZIRLO samples are plotted in Figure 3, which shows that bending moment is a strong function of cladding oxidation that occurs after rupture. For samples oxidized to 10–18 percent CP-ECR, the best-fit linear correlation to the data is given by the following:

$$M_{max} = 13.96 - 1.090 \ (CP\text{-}ECR - 10\%), \ N\bullet m \quad\quad\quad (1)$$

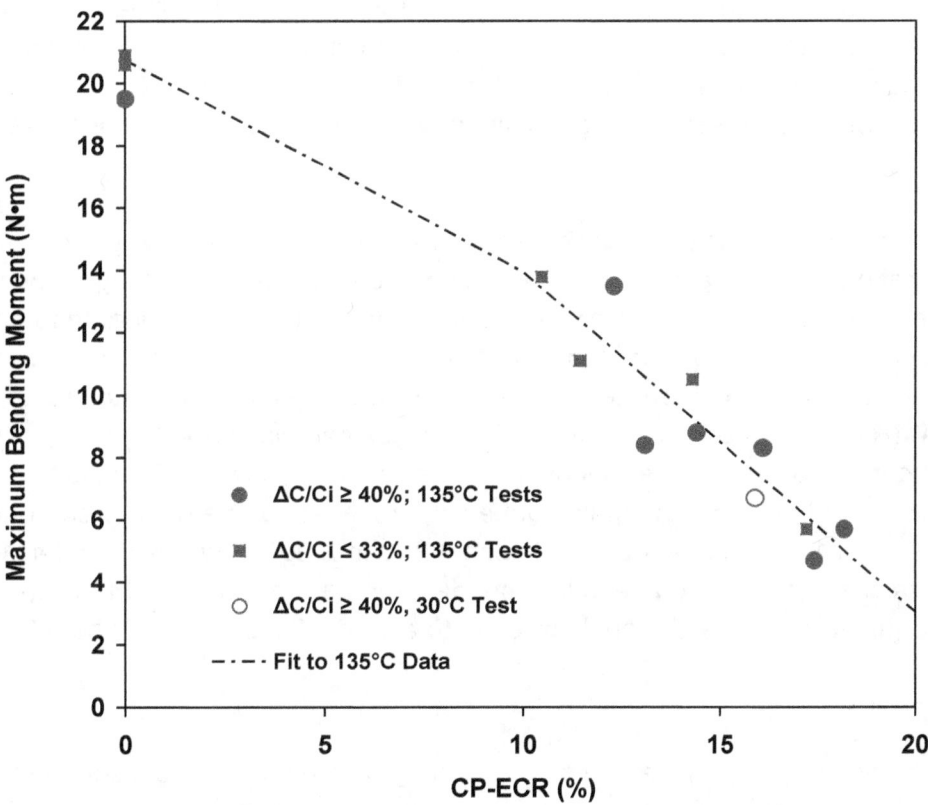

Figure 3 Maximum bending moment as a function of maximum oxidation level (CP-ECR) for post-LOCA samples subjected to 4-PBTs with the rupture region in tension for all tests but one. Bend tests were performed at 135 °C and 2 or 1 mm/s to 14-mm maximum displacement. One bend test was performed at 30 °C and 1 mm/s.

At the current licensing limit of 17 percent, Equation 1 gives 6.3 newton meters (N•m) as the failure bending moment. Measured values at 17 percent CP-ECR were 4.7 N•m (49 percent rupture strain) and 5.7 N•m (24 percent rupture strain). The correlation goes to zero at about 23 percent CP-ECR, which is physically unrealistic because failure requires $M_{max} > 0$ N•m. It is more probable that the failure bending moment decreases gradually to very small values with increasing CP-ECR. The results strongly suggest that oxidation in the balloon region should be limited to maintain geometric integrity of the cladding during and following quench in response to loads (e.g., axial loads due to partial axial-contraction restraint) beyond the quench-induced thermal stresses for unconstrained cladding.

In order to achieve low oxidation levels, with a maximum oxidation temperature of 1,200 degrees C, it was necessary to increase the average preoxidation cladding wall thickness by lowering the rupture strain to about 20 percent. This change made the rupture opening stronger than the higher hydrogen regions, in which severing then occurred. Similar results were obtained for all samples with less than or equal to 32 percent rupture strain.

Based on the results of one room temperature (RT) 4-PBT (see OCZL#32 test sample at 16 percent CP-ECR), the maximum bending moment appears to be relatively insensitive to test temperature. This result is quite different from the RCT ductility results, which indicated that permanent and offset strains were strong functions of test temperature (135 degrees C versus RT).

The 4-PBT strength results appear to be a meaningful measure of cladding performance; however, application of these results to LOCA acceptance criteria is not straightforward. Bending moments and axial bending stresses during quench are not anticipated to be significantly large, especially compared to potential axial stresses from partial contraction restraint. Test results from axial tensile tests test performed by the Japan Atomic Energy Agency (JAEA) (Ref. 16, 18-20) indicate that the samples can withstand high axial tensile loads without severing if the oxidation level is limited. Under full axial restraint, results from tests conducted by JAEA indicate that the maximum axial force that can be generated during quench following oxidation at 1,200 degrees C is between 1,200 to 2,000 newtons (N) (Ref. 16, 18-20). Appendix C to this report shows that a failure bending moment of about 6 N•m (from Equation 1 with CP-ECR equal to 17 percent) would correlate to an axial failure load of about 2,500 N.

4.1.2 Failure Energy

The failure or maximum (when no failure occurs) energy is plotted versus oxidation level in Figure 4, which shows that the failure energy is also a strong function of cladding oxidation that occurs after rupture. Load-displacement results from ramp-to-rupture tests (zero percent CP-ECR) were used to determine upper-bound energies of about 8 joules (J) for unfailed samples through 14-mm displacement. Although this value does not represent the maximum energy that such samples could accumulate before failure, it does represent the maximum that can be accumulated through 14-mm displacement. As can be seen in Figure 4, there is a significant decrease in failure energy with an increase in oxidation level from 0 to 10 percent, although without data in this region, the details of this decrease are not clear. The decrease in failure energy is more gradual for increasing oxidation levels from 10 to 18 percent.

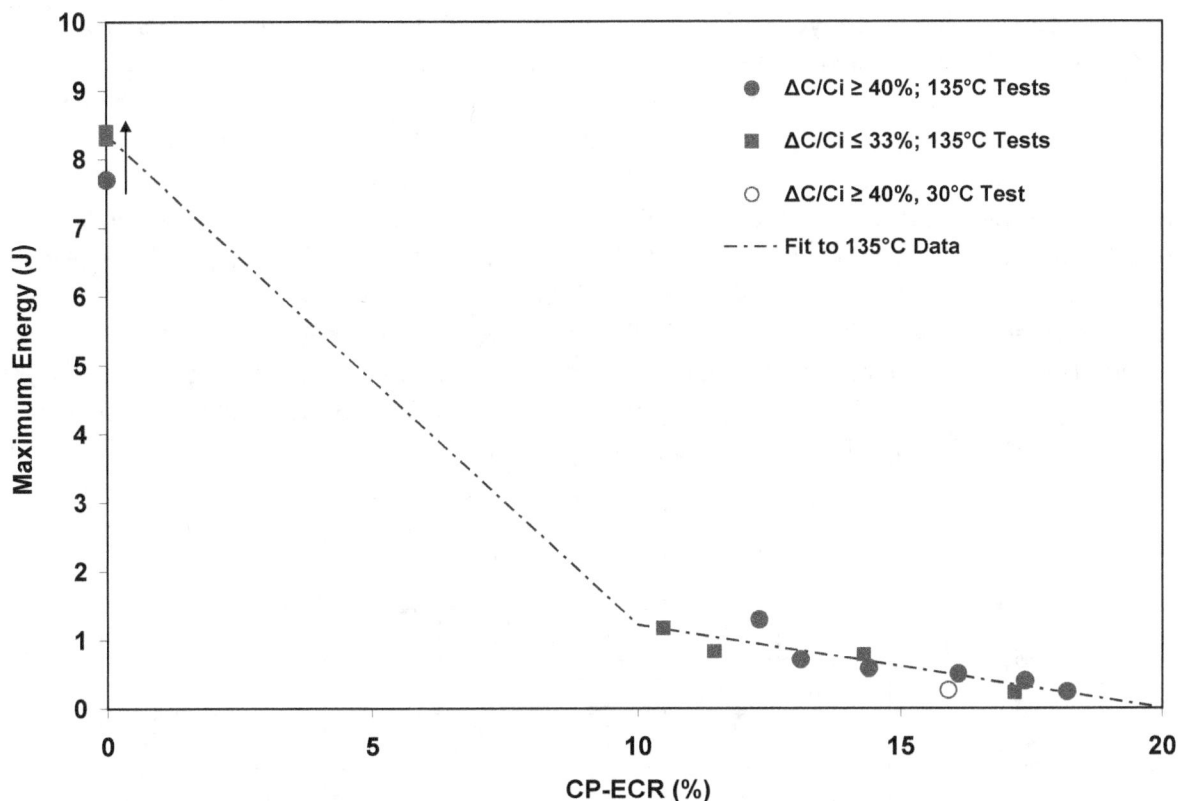

Figure 4 Maximum (for 0% CP-ECR) and failure (for ≥10% CP-ECR) energy as a function of oxidation level (CP-ECR) for post-LOCA samples subjected to four-point bending with the rupture region in tension for all tests but one. Bend tests were performed at 135 °C and 2 or 1 mm/s to 14-mm maximum displacement. One bend test was conducted at 30 °C and 1 mm/s.

The best-fit linear correlation for failure energy versus CP-ECR in the range of 10 to 18 percent oxidation level is given by Equation 2:

$$E_{max} = 1.22 - 0.121 \, (CP\text{-}ECR - 10\%), \, J \qquad (2)$$

The failure energy represented by Equation 2 gives 0.25 J at 18 percent CP-ECR (limit of database) and near zero at about 20 percent CP-ECR. Although it is physically unrealistic for the failure energy to go to zero, it clearly becomes very small at high oxidation levels. In order to maintain some toughness, the oxidation level should be limited.

4.1.3 Offset Displacement

Offset displacement is a measure of plastic displacement. The post-LOCA 4-PBT load-displacement curves give three types of results in terms of offset displacement: (1) severing with zero offset displacement in brittle regions outside the rupture node, (2) severing with zero offset displacement in brittle-to-ductile regions of the rupture cross section, and (3) partial-wall, brittle cracking followed by ductile crack growth during which offset strain is observed.

For the ramp-to-rupture samples (zero percent CP-ECR), there was a smooth transition between the constant load-displacement slope in the elastic bending regime and the decreasing slope after initiation of plastic flow in the axial direction, as can be seen in Figure 5. Measured offset displacements were in the range of 7 to 8 mm for these ductile samples. The loading stiffness values were reasonably close, but they appeared to increase somewhat with decreasing rupture strain: 120 N/mm for 69 percent rupture strain, 130 N/mm for 33 percent rupture strain, and 135 N/mm for 21 percent rupture strain.

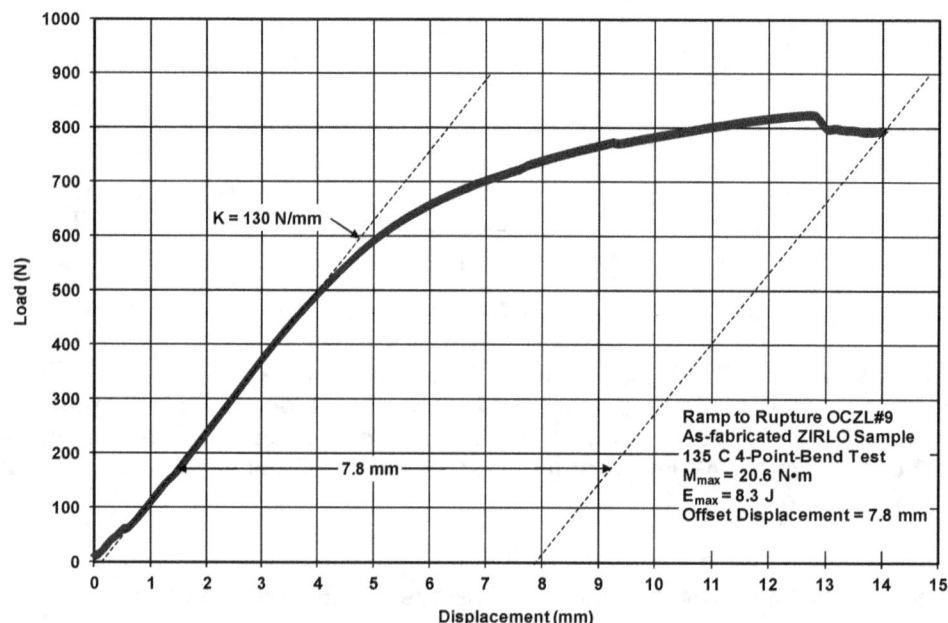

Figure 5 Four-point bend test load-displacement curve for ramp-to-rupture sample OCZL#9. The as-fabricated ZIRLO sample ruptured at 875±15 °C with a mid-wall rupture strain of 33%. The 4-PBT was conducted at 135 °C and 2 mm/s displacement rate to 14-mm maximum displacement.

The load-displacement curves for oxidized samples were quite different from the ones for ramp-to-rupture samples. It is clear from these tests at less than or equal to 18 percent CP-ECR that a significant fraction of the cladding cross section in the rupture node has plasticity; yet most of these tests show no offset displacement. Most samples (seven out of nine quenched samples) severed with an abrupt load drop during the linear portion of the loading ramp. These seven samples exhibited no offset displacement before crack initiation and propagation through the cross section. Five of these samples failed outside the rupture node and two failed in the rupture node.

Offset displacement appears to be affected by balloon size, loading history, loading orientation, and other factors not yet quantified. Well-behaved trends are not observed as they are for bending moment and failure energy. Therefore, although offset displacement is related to ductility, it is not a useful metric for behavior of the balloon region.

4.1.4 Failure Location

As mentioned earlier, research reported in the early 1980s in both the U.S. (NRC) and Japan (Japan Atomic Energy Research Institute) found regions of high hydrogen concentration just above and below the rupture location. This was a consequence of oxidation of the inside cladding surface by steam, which enters through the rupture opening. Research in both countries found that these neck regions in the balloon could be brittle. These are regions in a balloon in which ductility may not be maintained even if the acceptance criteria in 10 CFR 50.46 are satisfied. Therefore, the location of failure within the ballooned and ruptured region of a fuel rod is significant in evaluating the appropriateness of a local oxidation criterion in the ballooned and ruptured region of the fuel rod. If failure consistently occurred at a location of high hydrogen and was independent of the local oxidation in the rupture node, then a local oxidation criterion in the ballooned and ruptured region of the fuel rod could be said to not provide appropriate indication of the degradation of mechanical behavior in this region during a LOCA. The location of failure during bend testing observed in the NRC's integral LOCA research program will be discussed below.

The five samples that severed outside the rupture node with zero offset strain all had rupture strains less than or equal to 32 percent and CP-ECR values in the range of 10 to 17 percent. A metallographic analysis for one of these samples (from Test OCZL#19) was performed at one of two severed cross sections and the hydrogen content was determined. Figure 6 shows the results of the post-bend characterizations. The primary failure occurred at 24 mm below the rupture midspan with 530-wppm hydrogen and 12 percent ECR.

The two samples that severed in the rupture node with zero offset strain had rupture strains greater than or equal to 40 percent and CP-ECR values of 12 and 18 percent. Figure 7 shows (a) the hydrogen distribution, (b) the severed sample, and (c) the cross section at the severed location for the OCZL#18 sample. The average CP-ECR was only 12 percent, and the hydrogen pickup at the failure location was negligible. For a ring with no rupture-opening flaw and uniform oxidation around the circumference, the sample would have exhibited high ductility (30 to 50 percent). However, the local oxidation for this sample varied from much greater than 35 percent at the rupture tips (see Figure 8a) to 10 percent at the thick back region 180° from the center of the rupture opening (see Figure 8b). Under tensile bending stress, the crack initiated at the brittle rupture tips and propagated rapidly through the cross section with no indication of offset displacement. Although it required a relatively high bending moment and energy to sever this sample, the "ductile" regions of the cladding did not have enough fracture toughness to blunt crack growth.

17

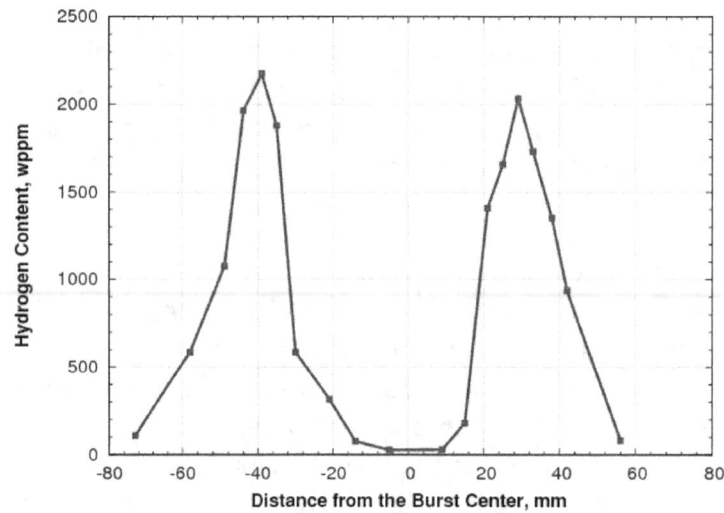

(a) Hydrogen-content profile

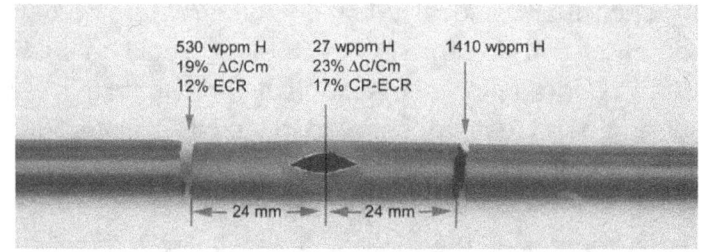

(b) Measured values at failure locations

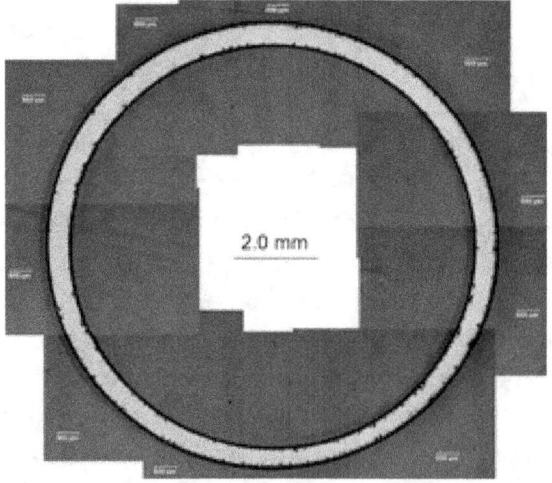

(c) Low-magnification image of severed cross section at -24 mm

Figure 6 Post-bend characterization of the OCZL#19 sample that was subjected to bending at 135 °C with the rupture region under maximum tensile stress: (a) hydrogen-content profile, (b) measured values at failure locations, and (c) low-magnification image of severed cross section at 24 mm below rupture midspan.

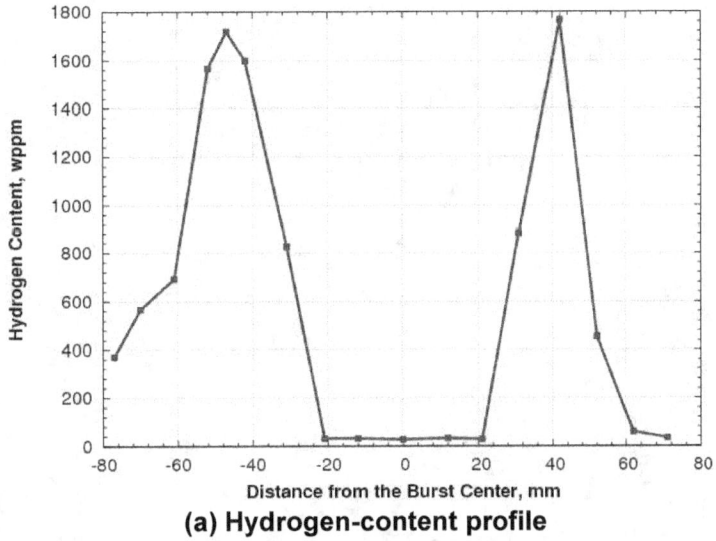

(a) Hydrogen-content profile

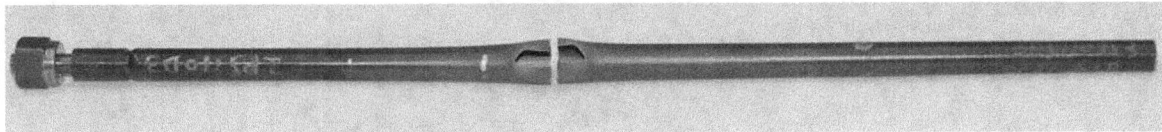

(b) Failure location

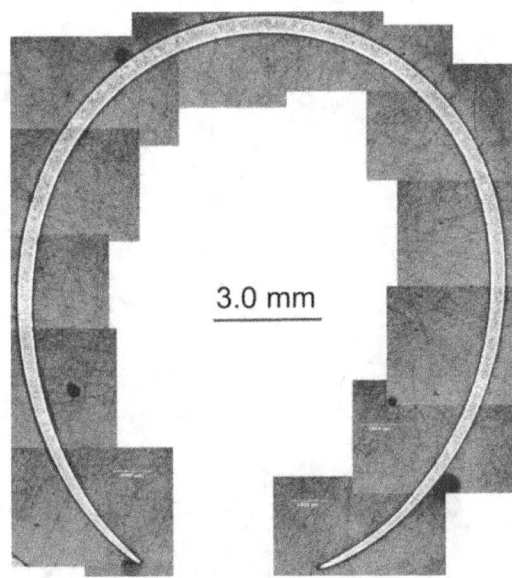

3.0 mm

(c) Low-magnification image of severed cross section

Figure 7 **Post-bend characterization of the OCZL#18 sample oxidized to 12% CP-ECR, quenched, and subjected to bending at 135 °C with the rupture region under maximum tensile stress: (a) hydrogen-content profile, (b) failure location, and (c) low-magnification image of the severed cross section.**

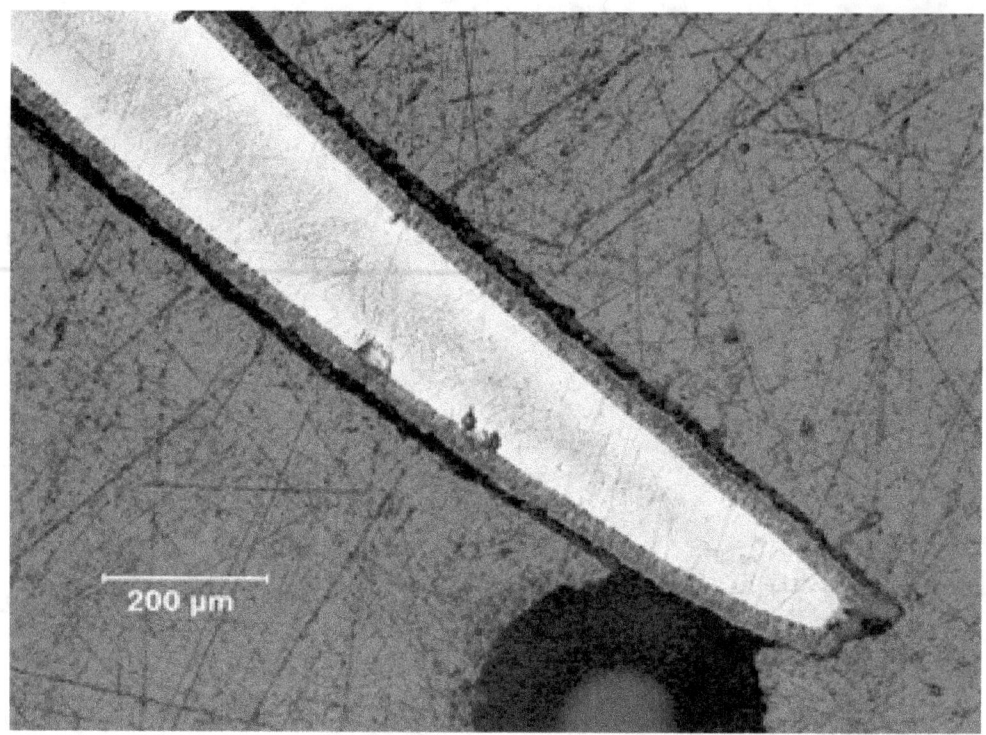

(a) Rupture tip

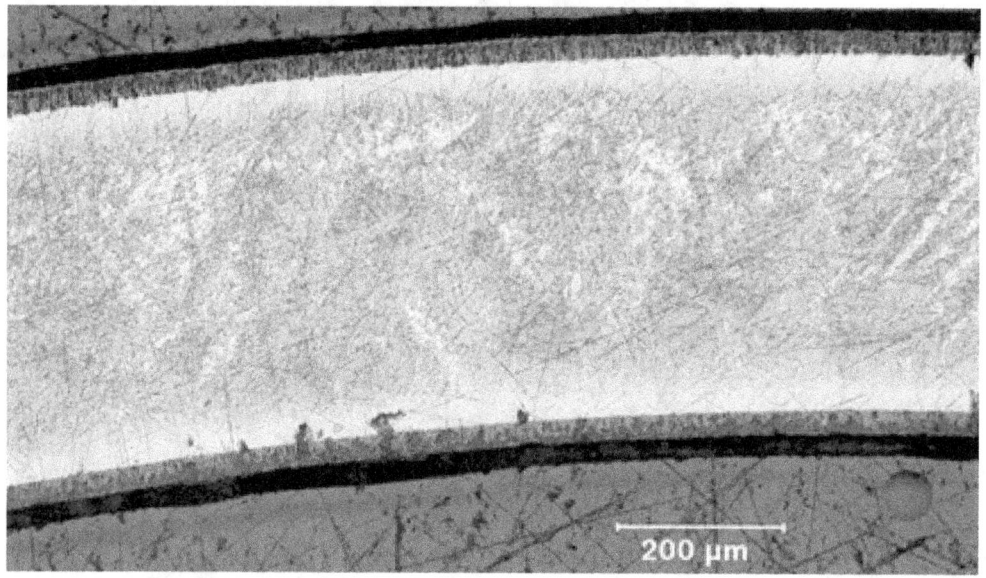

(b) Back side of rupture node cross section

Figure 8 Metallographic images for the OCZL#18 severed cross section following oxidation to 12% CP-ECR, quench, and bending at 135 °C with the rupture region under maximum tension: (a) rupture tip with 0.14-mm average metal wall and (b) back side of cross section with 0.44-mm metal wall thickness.

Figure 9 shows the results of the post-bend characterization of a sample that was tested with the rupture opening in compression (OCZL#12). This sample had an average oxidation of 14 percent CP-ECR in the rupture node, and the primary failure occurred at 40 mm below the rupture midspan with 1,700-wppm hydrogen and 8 percent ECR. However, severing of the sample at 33 mm above the rupture midspan appears to be an equally probable failure location based on hydrogen content and oxidation level. Figure 10 shows the OCZL#15 sample, which was another sample subjected to reverse bending (rupture region under compression), after oxidation to 18 percent CP-ECR and cooling without quench. The offset strain for this intact sample was 13 mm.

Figure 11 shows the OCZL#17 sample, which was subjected to standard bending (rupture region under tension). The back region of the cladding remained intact after 10-mm displacement with an offset displacement of 6.3 mm. In Figure 11a, the load-displacement curve is truncated at 4-mm displacement. From 4- to 10-mm displacement, the load remained quite low (3 to 13 N) as the ductile ligament at the back of the cladding deformed plastically. This ductile deformation region contributed about 10 percent to the maximum energy. The OCZL#29 sample was also subjected to the standard ANL bend test. This test was terminated after about 3-mm displacement (Figure 12) and reloaded (Figure 13). Cracking began at a relatively low load (188 N) and bending moment (4.7 N•m). The load dropped rather abruptly from 188 N to 107 N and again from 124 N to 85 N. At the end of these two load drops, the crack had propagated across more than half the cross section. After reloading, the crack continued to propagate in a ductile manner, leaving only the back region intact.

In summary, the location of failure within the ballooned and ruptured region under four-point bending was found to occur in either the middle of the rupture node, where local oxidation was greatest, or in a region of high hydrogen content above and/or below the rupture node. The location of failure appeared to be influenced by the balloon size. However, even when fracture occurred away from the center of the rupture region, where significant hydrogen absorption took place during high temperature oxidation, the bending moment and failure energy were still shown to decrease with increasing oxidation to a degree consistent with samples that failed in the center of the rupture region. This can be seen in Figure 3 and Figure 4, where the bending moments and failure energy of samples that failed in the rupture node or outside of the rupture node are plotted together. For the most part, tests conducted on segments with greater than or equal to 40 percent balloon strain failed in the rupture node, while tests conducted on segments with less than or equal to 33 percent balloon strain failed outside of the rupture node, yet no obvious trend is observed to differentiate these two data sets. This suggests that limiting oxidation preserves mechanical behavior in the ballooned and ruptured region of a fuel rod, even when additional degradation mechanisms beyond localized oxidation are present.

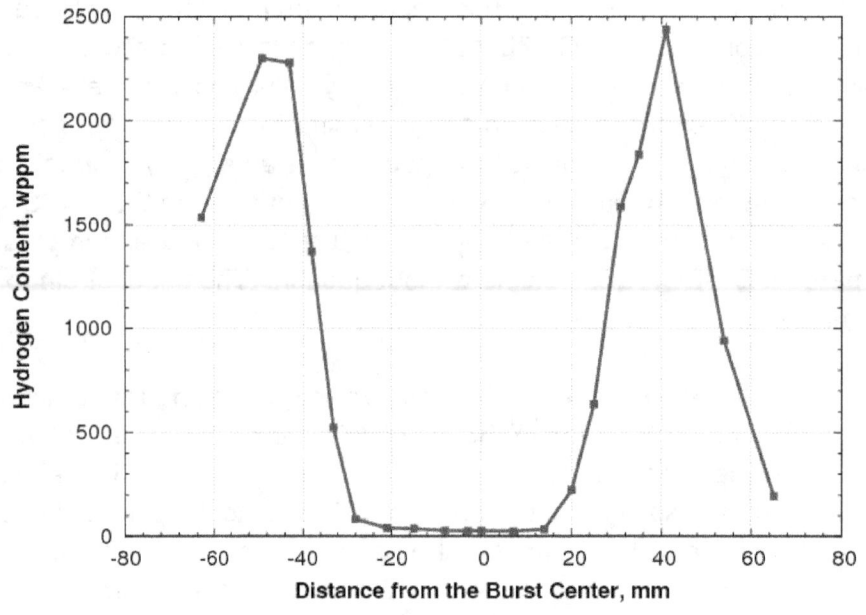

(a) Hydrogen-content profile

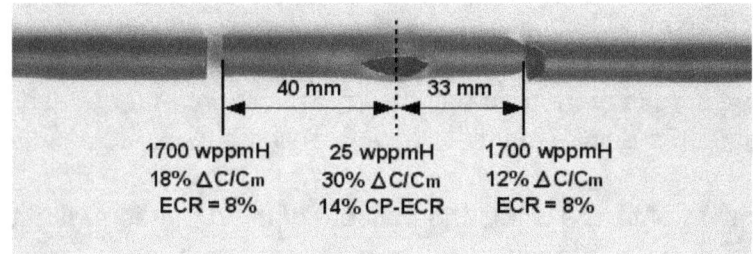

(b) Measured values at failure locations

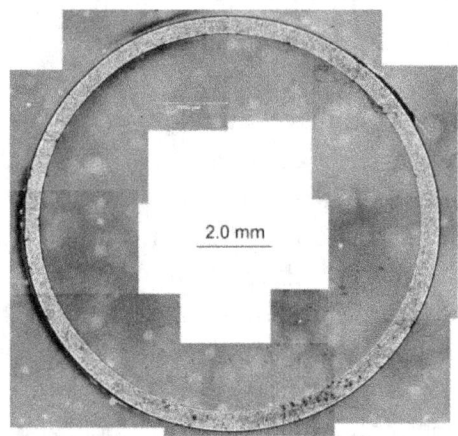

(c) Low-magnification image of severed cross section at -40 mm

Figure 9 Post-bend characterization of OCZL#12 sample that was subjected to bending at 135 °C with the rupture region under maximum compressive stress: (a) hydrogen-content profile, (b) measured values at failure locations, and (c) low-magnification image of severed cross section at 40 mm below rupture midspan.

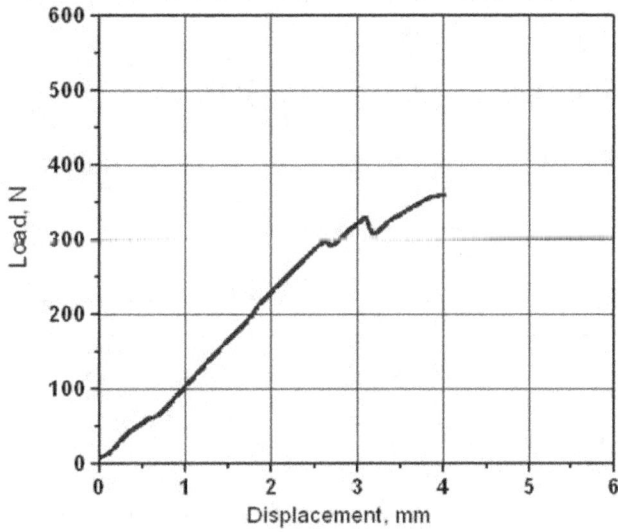

(a) First loading

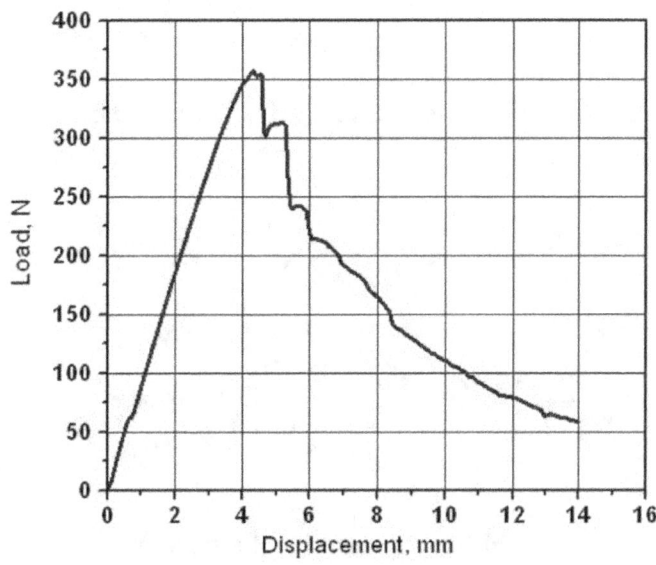

(b) Second loading

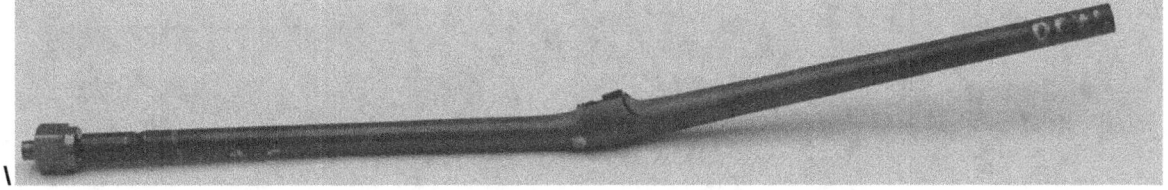

(c) Sample appearance after second loading

Figure 10 Post-bend results for the OCZL#15 sample (18% CP-ECR and quench) with rupture node in compression (reverse bending), 135 °C test temperature and 2 mm/s displacement rate: (a) load-displacement curve for first loading and (b) load-displacement curve for second loading.

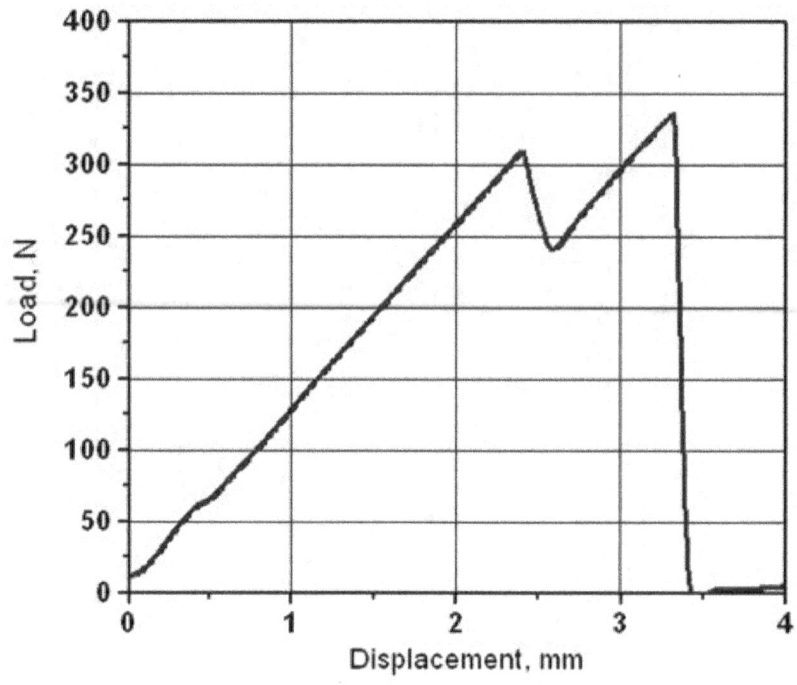

(a) Load-displacement curve for first 4-mm displacement

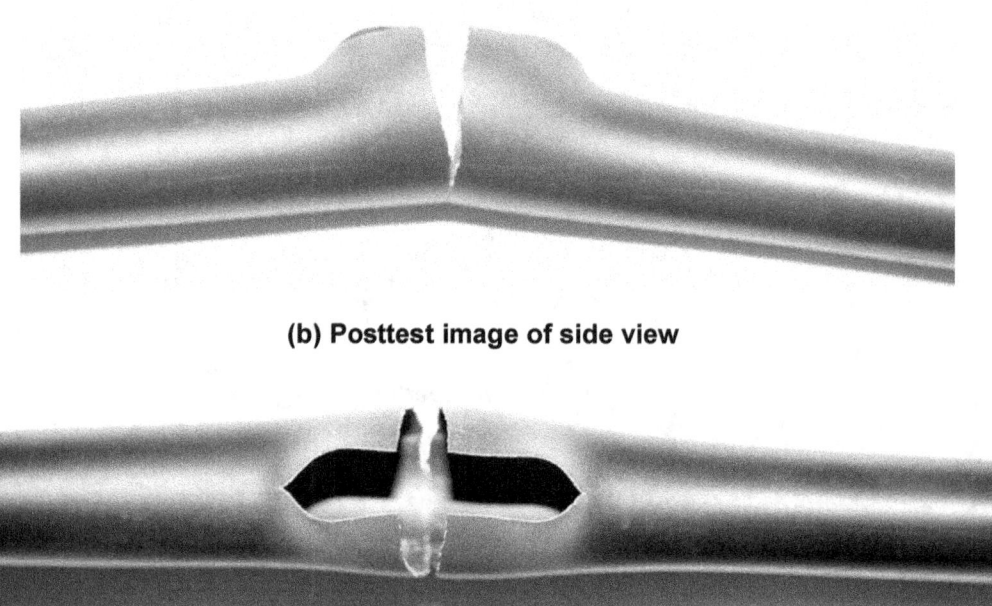

(b) Posttest image of side view

(c) Posttest image of rupture view

Figure 11 4-PBT results for Test Sample OCZL#17 oxidized to 13% CP-ECR, quenched, and tested at 135 °C and 2 mm/s displacement rate: (a) load-displacement curve for first 4-mm displacement (out of 10-mm total displacement, (b) posttest image of side view, and (c) posttest image of rupture view.

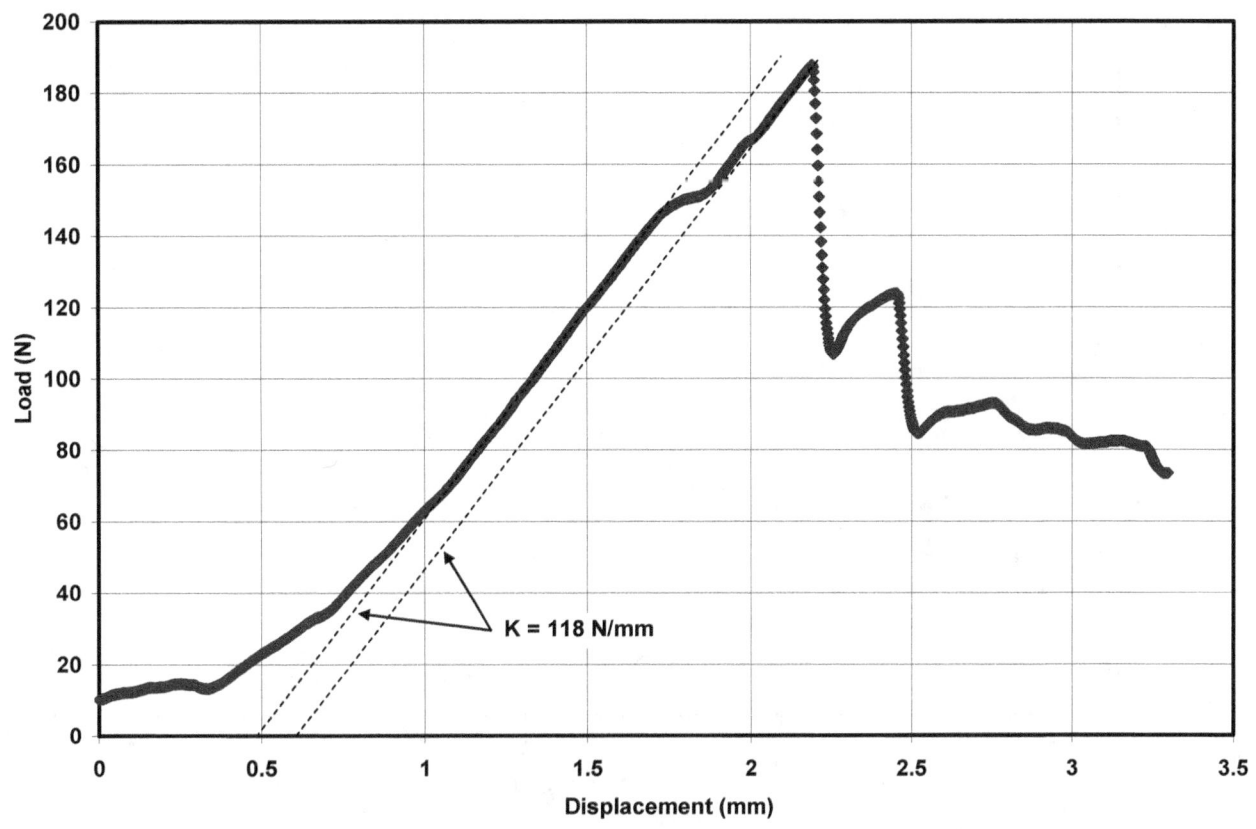

(a) First loading-unloading sequence

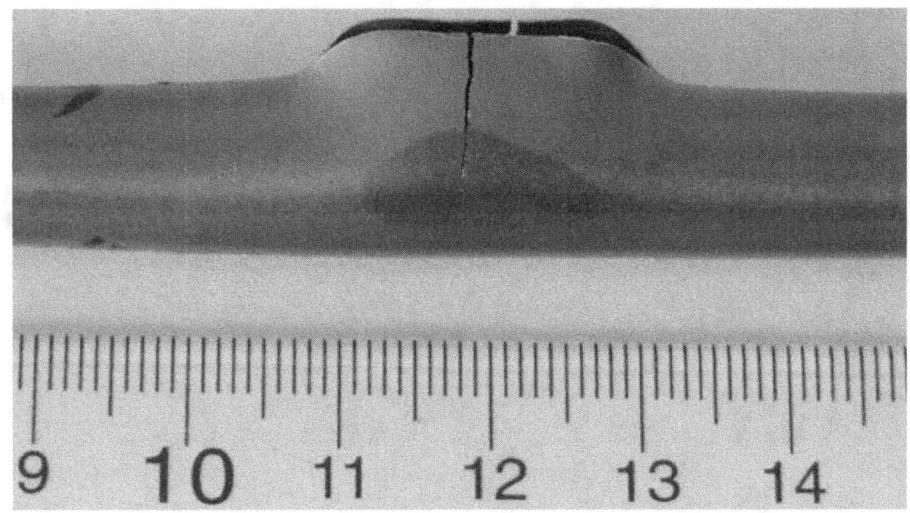

(b) Side view after first loading-unloading

Figure 12 Test Sample OCZL#29 oxidized to 17% CP-ECR, quenched, and subjected to 4-PBTs at 135 °C and 1 mm/s displacement rate: (a) load-displacement curve for first loading-unloading sequence and (b) sample appearance after first loading-unloading.

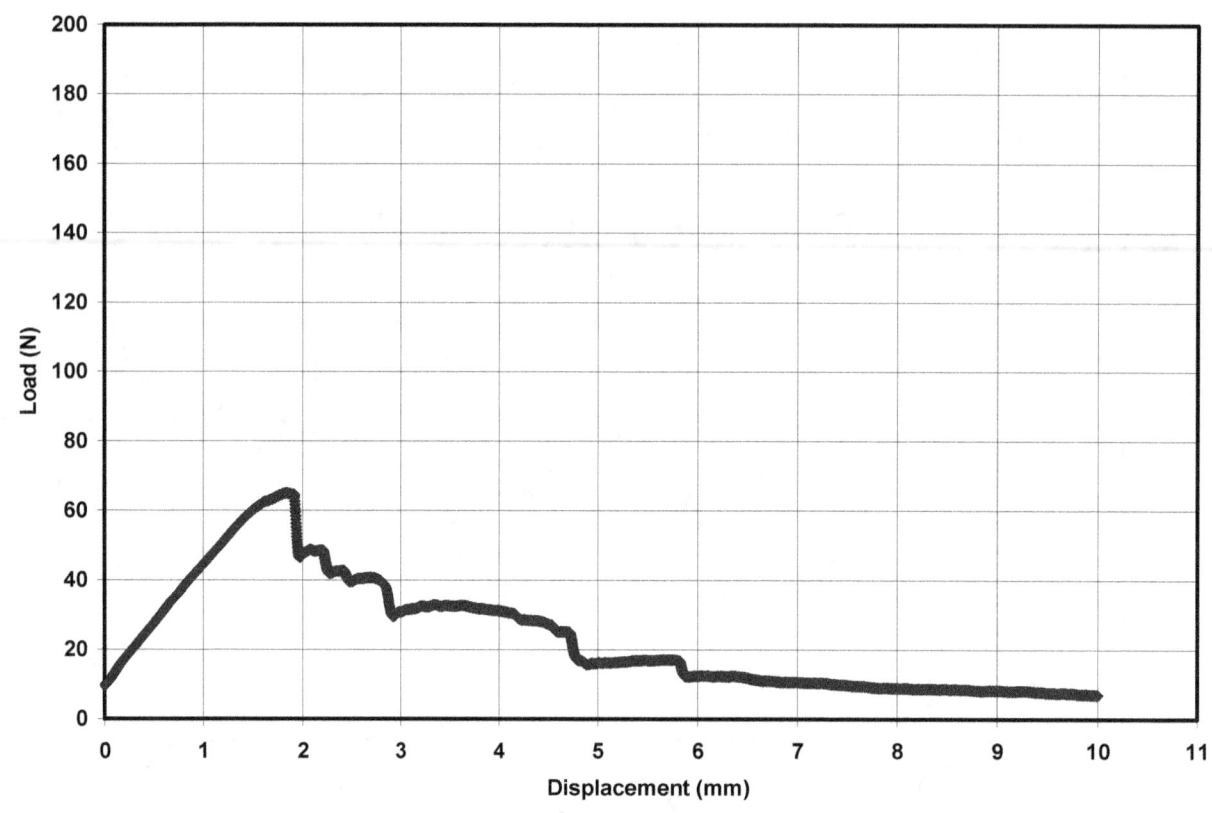

(a) Second loading-unloading

(b) Rupture view after second loading-unloading

Figure 13 Test Sample OCZL#29 oxidized to 17% CP-ECR, quenched, and subjected to 4-PBTs at 135 °C and 1 mm/s displacement rate: (a) load-displacement curve for second loading-unloading sequence and (b) sample appearance after second loading-unloading.

4.2 Results of Testing of Irradiated Cladding Material

Irradiated, high-burnup cladding material was tested at Studsvik. Benchmarking[2] and characterization tests were conducted at Studsvik with as-received cladding material in order to validate the test device and procedures, as well as to confirm that the results of tests at Studsvik were directly comparable to results of parallel tests at ANL. Following benchmarking and characterization, four tests on fuel segments taken from high-burnup Westinghouse ZIRLO rods with burnups of 70–73 megawatt days per kilogram of uranium (MWD/kgU) were conducted at Studsvik. Of these four tests, three accumulated nonnegligible high-temperature oxidation, while the fourth was a ramp-to-rupture test terminated just after rupture and before significant high temperature oxidation. Test 189 was a ramp-to-rupture test, Test 191 was a full-sequence LOCA test with a target CP-ECR level of 12 percent, Test 192 was a full-sequence LOCA test with a target CP-ECR level of 10 percent, and Test 193 was a full-sequence LOCA test with a target CP-ECR level of about 17 percent. In this section, details of rod selection, the LOCA simulation, and posttransient conditions will be discussed for each of the four tests, along with the results of the 4-PBT for each test segment. Additional information on the analysis of the Studsvik results is available in a letter report from ANL (Ref. 15).

4.2.1 Rod Selection: Burnup, Eddy Current, and Hydrogen Measurements

For each of the four tests, a segment of high-burnup Westinghouse ZIRLO™ was used. The segments were taken from rods that were irradiated in a U.S commercial power plant and had a rod average burnup between 70 and 73 MWD/kgU. Each segment was 300 mm in length. The hydrogen content was measured just above each segment. The eddy current measurements indicate that the initial oxide layer thickness was relatively constant over the length of this segment.

4.2.2 Details of the Simulation: Cladding Temperature and Rod Pressure History

For Test 189, the simulation was run through ballooning and rupture, and the test was terminated at 950 degrees C. The furnace was shut off to terminate the test and there was no quench. No significant oxidation was accumulated during this test. It serves as the "zero" CP-ECR reference point for 4-PBT results and was used to estimate balloon size for subsequent tests.

For Test 191, the simulation was run through ballooning and rupture and oxidized at a temperature set point of 1,160 degrees C for 25 seconds. Previous benchmarks indicated that the control thermocouple location is a relatively cold location and that a majority of the cladding circumference sees a slightly higher temperature than the thermocouple. The set point of 1,160 degrees C was selected, based on prior measurements, to provide an average cladding temperature in the range of 1,185 ±20 degrees C. The target CP-ECR for Test 191 was

---

[2] See Appendix B for a discussion of the benchmarking of 4-PBT results between ANL and Studsvik.

12 percent. This is the ECR at which the transition from ductile-to-brittle behavior was observed in RCTs for cladding material with 200-wppm hydrogen.

For Test 192, the simulation was run through ballooning and rupture, and the sample was oxidized at a temperature set point of 1,160 degrees C to a target CP-ECR of 10 percent.

For Test 193, the simulation was run through ballooning and rupture and oxidized at a temperature set point of 1,160 degrees C to target a CP-ECR of 17 percent.

Figure 14 indicates the time history of temperature and pressure. Rupture pressure and temperature are indicated in the title of each component of the figure.

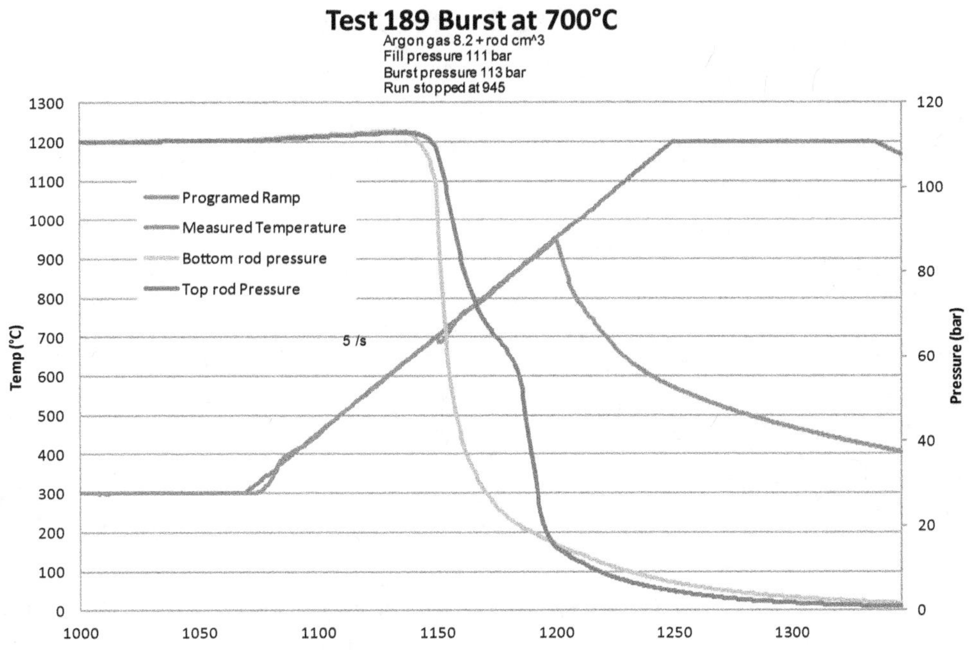

Test 189 Burst at 700°C
Argon gas 8.2 + rod cm^3
Fill pressure 111 bar
Burst pressure 113 bar
Run stopped at 945
Programed Ramp
Measured Temperature
Bottom rod pressure
Top rod Pressure
5 /s
Temp (°C)
Pressure (bar)
1300
1200
1100
1000
900
800
700
600
500
400
300
200
100
0
120
100
80
60
40
20
0
1000
1050
1100
1150
1200
1250
1300

(a)

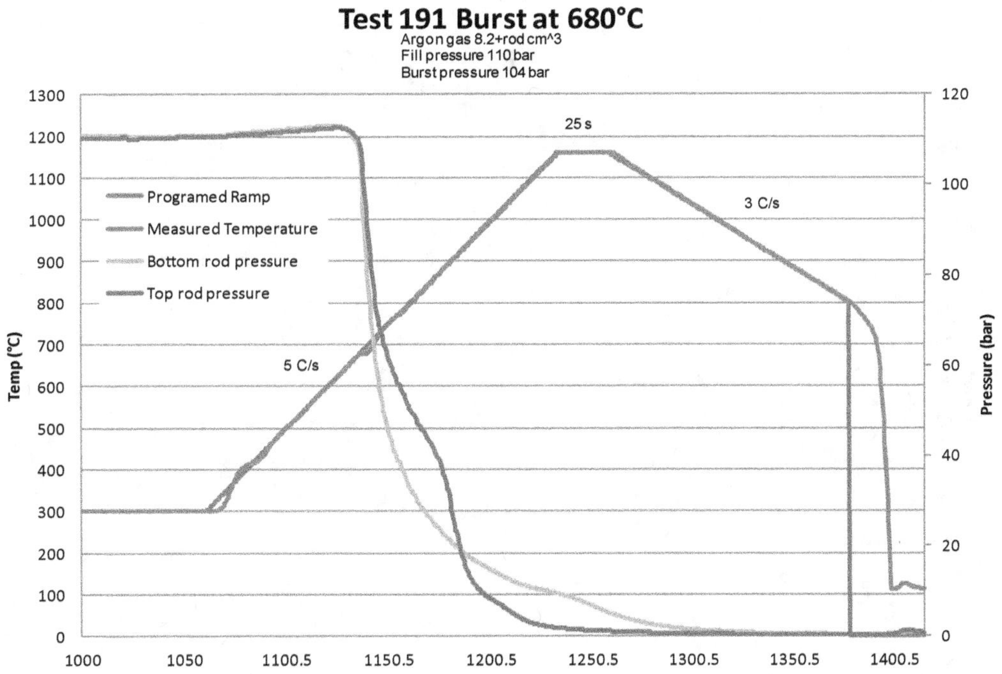

Test 191 Burst at 680°C
Argon gas 8.2+rod cm^3
Fill pressure 110 bar
Burst pressure 104 bar
Programed Ramp
Measured Temperature
Bottom rod pressure
Top rod pressure
25 s
3 C/s
5 C/s
Temp (°C)
Pressure (bar)
1300
1200
1100
1000
900
800
700
600
500
400
300
200
100
0
120
100
80
60
40
20
0
1000
1050
1100.5
1150.5
1200.5
1250.5
1300.5
1350.5
1400.5

(b)

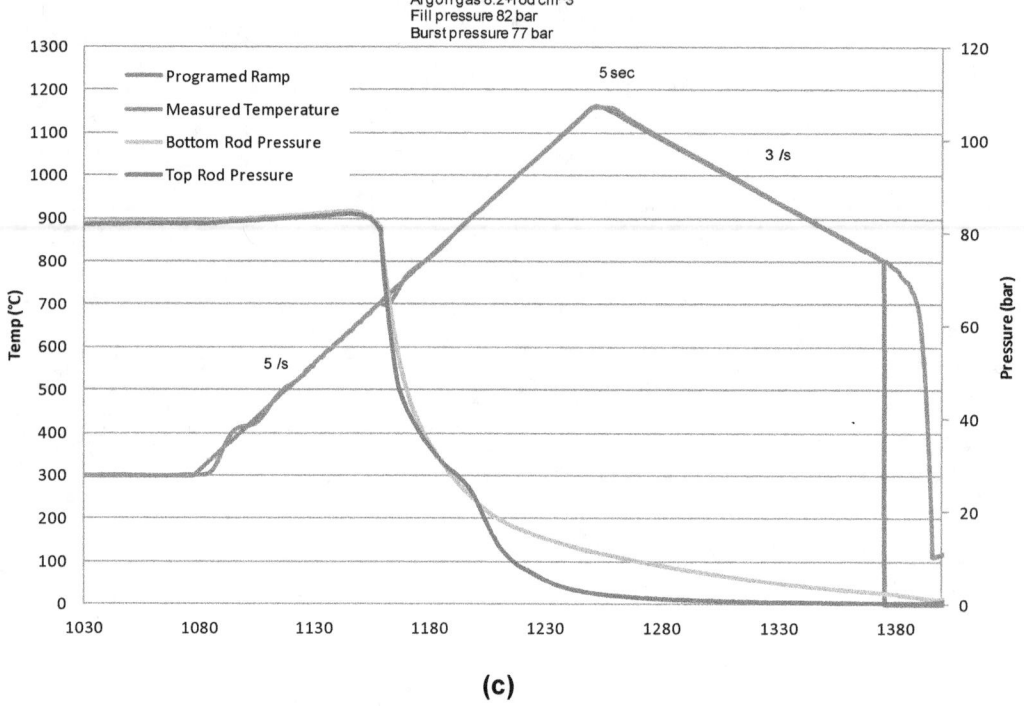

(c)

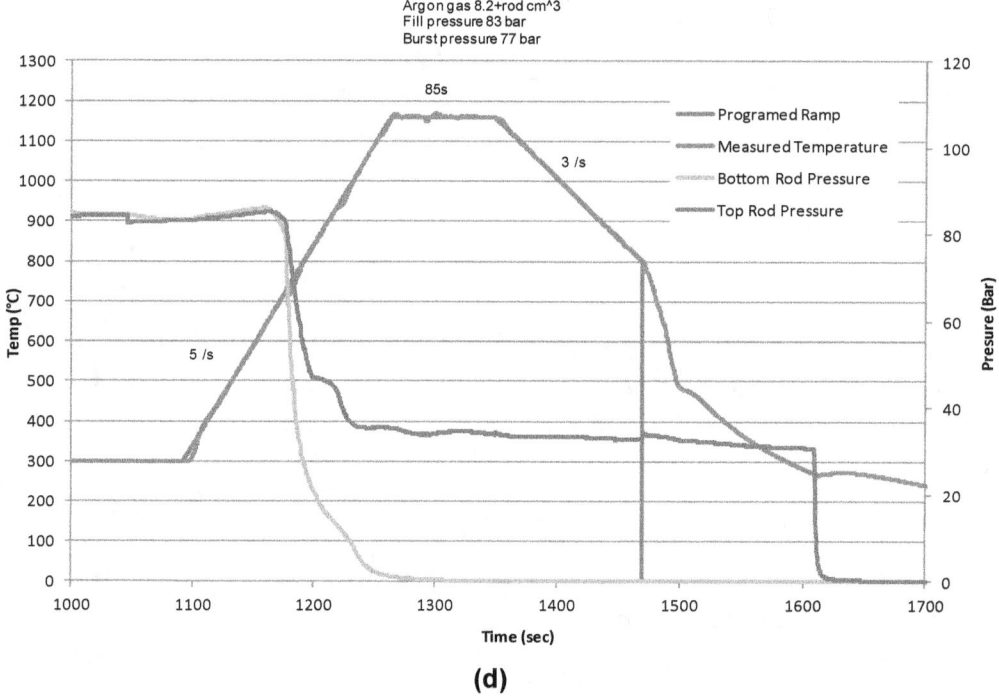

(d)

Figure 14 Temperature and pressure history for Test (a) 189, (b) 191, (c) 192, and (d) 193.

4.2.3 Posttransient Conditions: Rupture Shape and Size, Rod Distortion, and Profilometry

After the LOCA simulation was completed, the fuel rod was examined. Figure 15 provides photos of the rupture region of each fuel rod after the simulation (note that these images are not presented at a uniform scale). Table 3 provides the dimensions of the rupture opening for each test, along with the measured ballooning strain, ECR calculated according to this strain, and the rupture characteristics.

Table 3 Test Characteristics.

	Test 189	Test 191	Test 192	Test 193
Comments	Ramp to rupture test	Ramp to PCT, held for 25 s at PCT	Ramp to PCT, held for 5 s at PCT	Ramp to PCT, held for 85 s at PCT
Burnup (GWd/MTU)	≈ 72	≈ 71	≈ 72	≈ 71
PCT (°C)	950 ± 20	1185 ± 20	1185 ± 20	1185 ± 20
Calculated ECR (%)	≈ 0	13	11	17
Fill Pressure (bar)	110	110	82	82
Rupture Pressure (bar)	113	104	77	77
Rupture Temperature (°C)	700	680	700	728
Rupture Opening Width (mm)	10.5	17.5	9.0	13.8

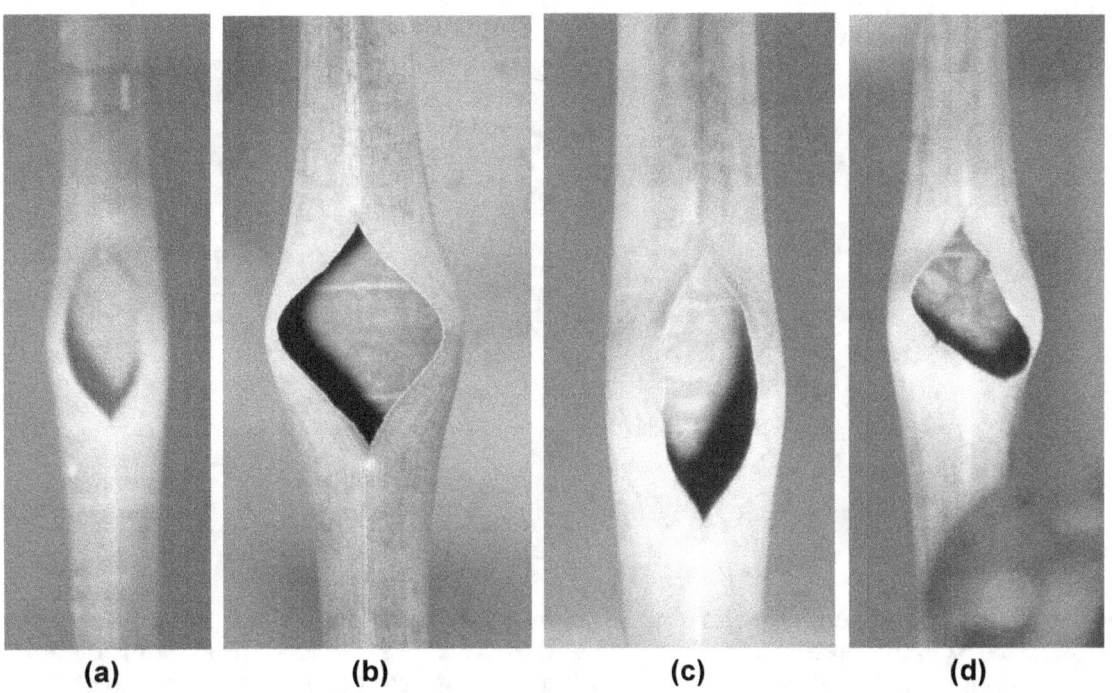

(a)   (b)   (c)   (d)

Figure 15 A closeup of the rupture opening after the simulation on rod segment from Test (a) 189, (b) 191, (c) 192, and (d) 193.

It is significant to note that, when the rupture opening was examined after the simulation, no fuel could be seen in the region. The observations of fuel loss in the Studsvik integral tests will be discussed elsewhere (Ref. 17).

During the LOCA simulation, one of the rod segments (the segment used in Test 191) experienced significant distortion in plane with the rupture opening. Another, from Test 193, experienced minor distortion in plane with the rupture opening. In both cases, the distortion seen in these tests is thought to be related to fuel fragments from previous tests that remained in the test train and around the o-ring and bottom plug. The presence of these fuel fragments increased the friction coefficient at this location and interfered with free expansion of the rod segment. None of the rod segments experienced distortion out of plane with the rupture, and the rod segments used in Tests 189 and 192 did not experience any distortion or bending during the LOCA simulation. Figure 16 provides images of any distortion present out of plane with the rupture for each test, in addition to one image taken of rod segment 189 in plane with the rupture, which is representative of all four tests.

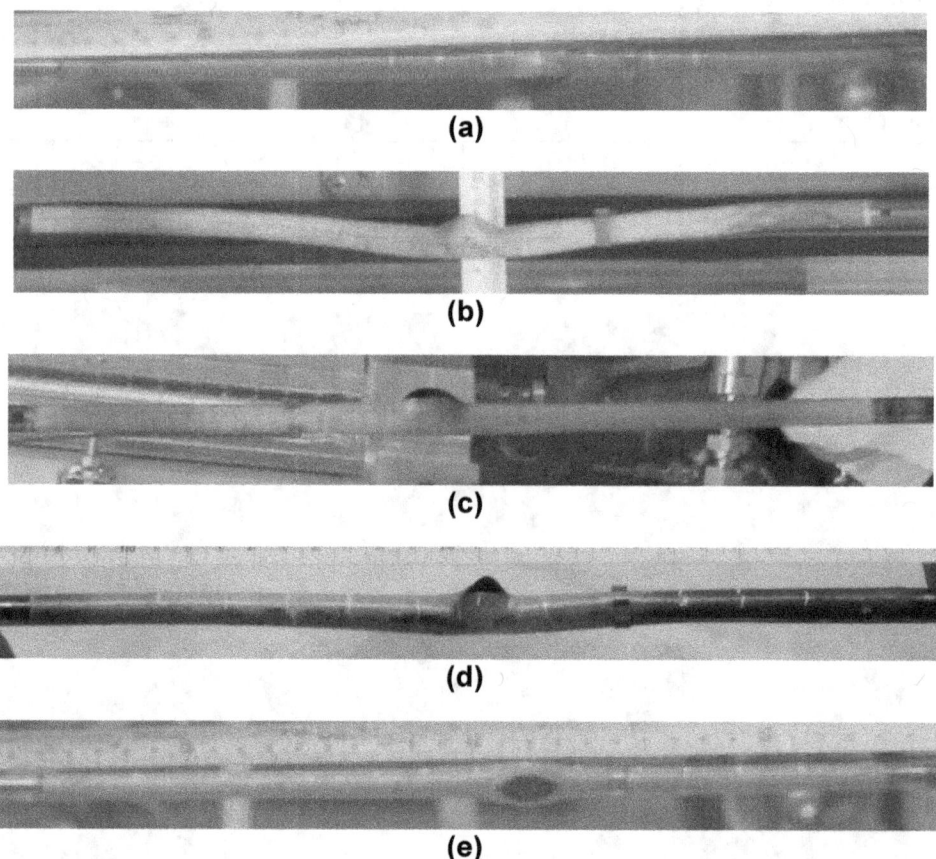

(a)

(b)

(c)

(d)

(e)

Figure 16 Image of rod segment showing any distortion out of plane, with the rupture from (a) Test 189, (b) Test 191, (c) Test 192, and (d) Test 193. (e) is an image of rod segment 189 taking in-plane of the rupture, showing no significant rod bending that is characteristics of all other tests.

Profilometry measurements were made of each rod segment following the LOCA simulation; they are shown in Figure 17. Figure 17 also indicates the initial diameter and burst length. See Table 3 above for the value of the midwall rupture strain calculated based on these data.

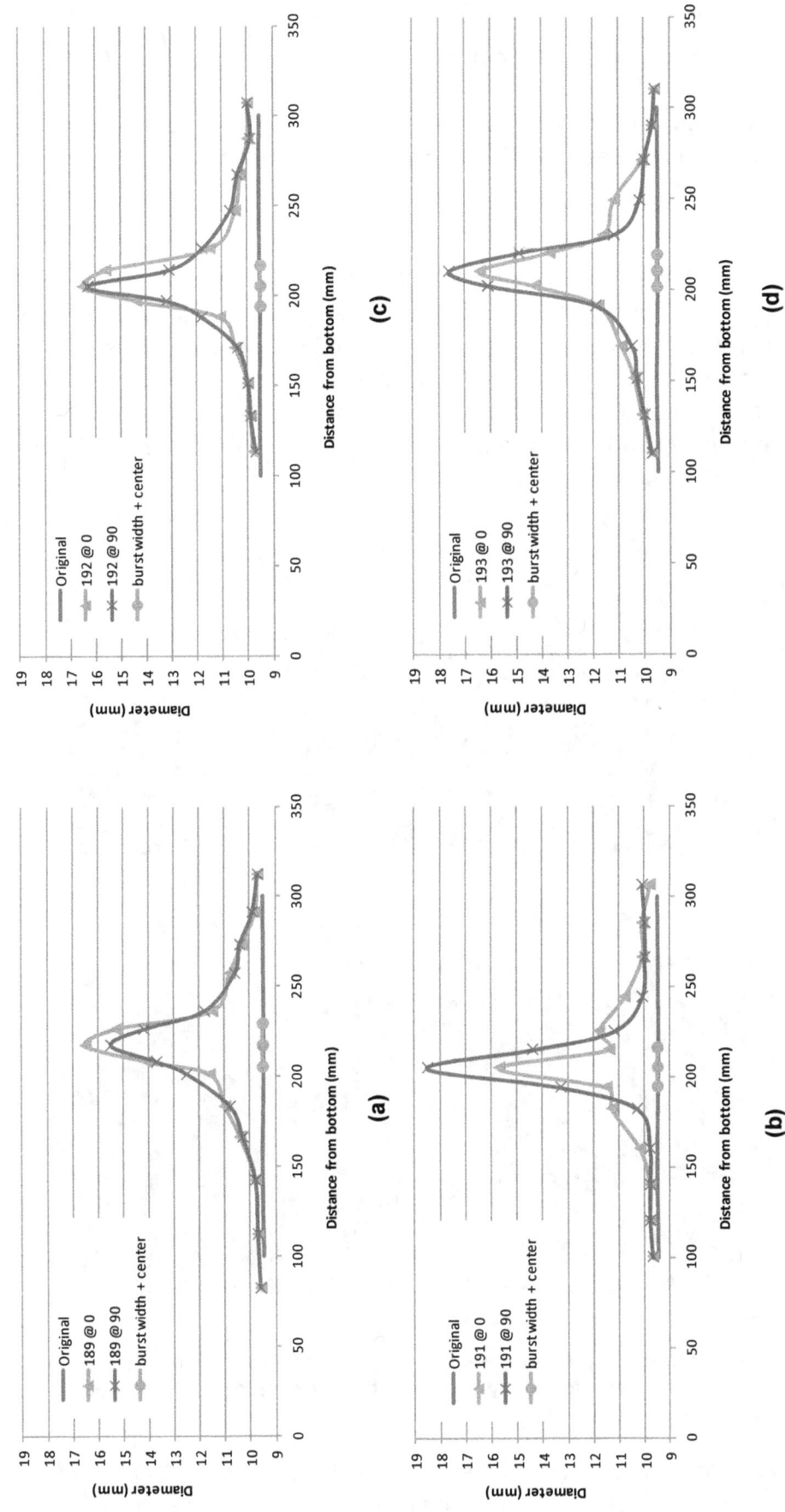

Figure 17 Profilometry measurements of segments (a) 189, (b) 191, (c) 192, and (d) 193, post-simulation. The burst length is also indicated.

4.2.4 Four-Point Bend Test: Before, After, Deflection, and Load Displacement

Following the LOCA simulation, each fuel rod segment was loaded in four-point bending. The results of the bend test for each fuel rod segment will be discussed individually.

4.2.4.1 Test 189

Figure 18 shows images before (a) and after (b) bending of test segment 189. The rod displayed highly ductile behavior and remained intact even after significant bending. Figure 19 illustrates the total displacement (a) by superimposing the initial and final images of the bent rod and (b) by revealing the entire segment length. It can be seen that the rod was able to bend nearly to a 90° angle without breaking. The deflection in this test was limited by the displacement range of the four-point bend device, and therefore it is possible that the rod would have been able to bend even further without breaking.

| (a) | (b) |

Figure 18 Rod segment 189 (a) before and (b) after four-point bending.

| (a) | (b) |

Figure 19 Illustrations indicating (a) the total displacement and (b) total bending of rod segment 189. Note that the deflection was limited by the bend device displacement range.

Figure 20 provides the load-displacement curve. The segment withstood over 1,200-N flexural load without breaking. The x-axis is flexural extension and indicates the displacement of the

34

loading pins. The displacement at the segment center is derived from this measurement. From the load-displacement curve, through 14.1-mm displacement, maximum values of load, bending moment, offset displacement at the loading pins, and energy were calculated to be 1,273 N, 31.8 N•m, 4.0 mm, and 10.4 J, respectively.

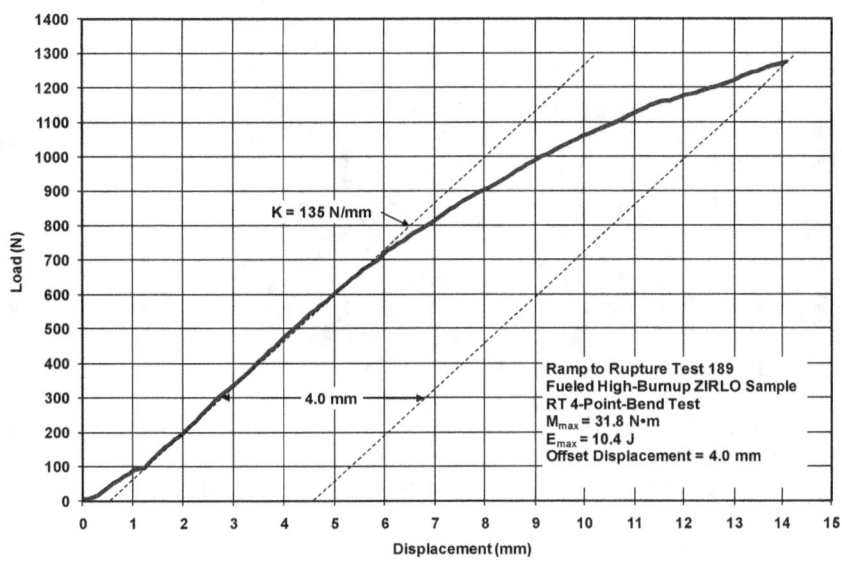

Figure 20 Load-displacement curve for the four-point bend test on segment 189.

4.2.4.2 Test 191

Figure 21 shows images before (a) and after (b) the bending and breaking of segment 191. The rod displayed fairly brittle behavior. Figure 22 shows the fracture profile for the fractured segment. It can be seen that the fracture path changed directions at the back, and that the original crack path extended after the main fracture path changed directions. It is significant to note that the fracture occurred near the center of the rupture region, at the location of maximum oxidation and minimum wall thickness. One of the objectives of this test series was to investigate if fracture occurred within the rupture region or in the highly hydrided "neck regions" Failure in the highly hydrided "neck regions" would indicate that these regions were more brittle and weaker than the highly oxidized rupture center.

(a)   (b)

Figure 21 Segment 191 (a) before and (b) after four-point bending.

35

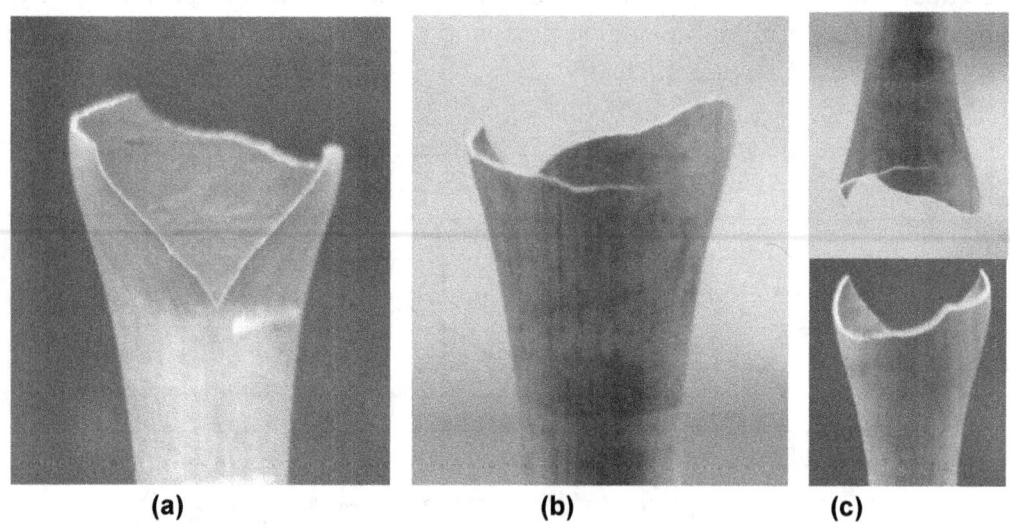

(a)	**(b)**	**(c)**

Figure 22 Images of the fracture profile from segment 191 after the four-point bend test: (a) the bottom half, (b) the top half, and (c) an illustration of the back side of the two halves put together. In (b) a second crack propagation path can be seen.

Figure 23 provides the load-displacement curve. The segment withstood over 300-N flexural load before breaking. The x-axis is flexural extension and indicates the displacement of the loading pins. From the load-displacement curve, values of maximum load, failure bending moment, offset displacement at the loading pins, and failure energy were calculated to be 307 N, 7.7 N•m, 0 mm, and 0.51 J, respectively.

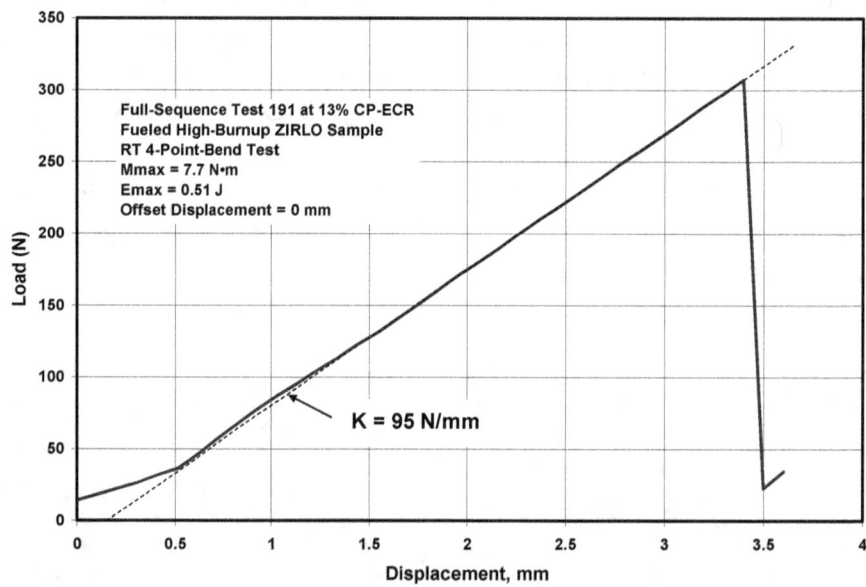

Figure 23 Load-displacement curve for the four-point bend test on segment 191.

4.2.4.3 Test 192

Figure 24 shows images (a) before and (b) after bending and breaking of rod segment 192. The rod displayed fairly brittle behavior. Figure 25 shows the fracture profile for the fractured segment. As in Test 191, the fracture occurred near the center of the rupture region, at the location of maximum oxidation and minimum wall thickness.

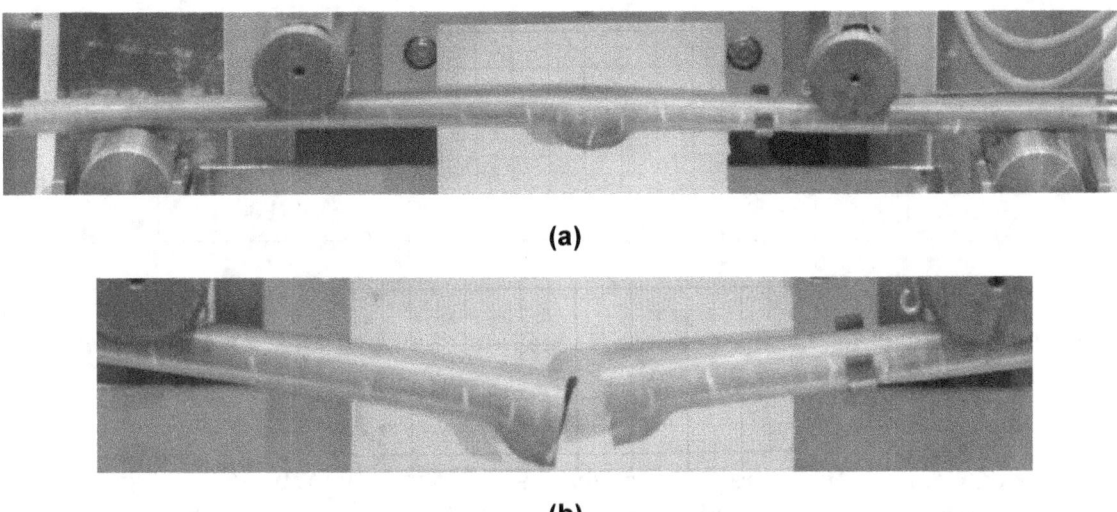

(a)

(b)

Figure 24 Segment 192 (a) before and (b) after four-point bending.

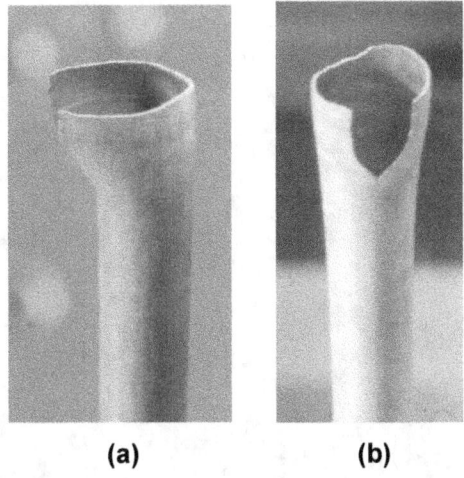

(a)   (b)

Figure 25 Images of the fracture profile from segment 192 after the four-point bend test.

Figure 26 provides the load-displacement curve. The segment withstood almost 400-N flexural load before breaking. The x-axis is flexural extension and indicates the displacement of the loading pins. From the load-displacement curve, values of maximum load, failure bending moment, offset displacement at the loading pins, and failure energy were calculated to be 400 N, 10.0 N•m, 0 mm, and 0.57 J, respectively.

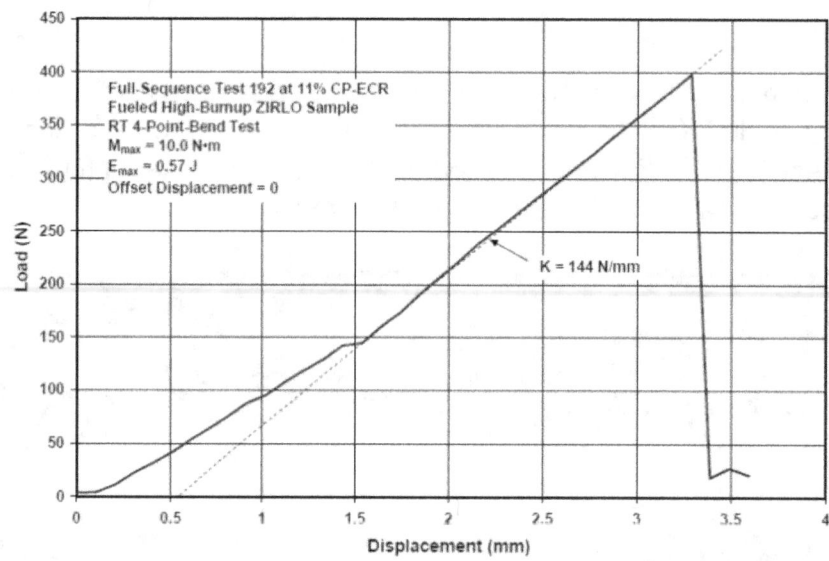

Figure 26 Load-displacement curve for the four-point bend test on segment 192.

4.2.4.4 Test 193

Following the LOCA simulation, the fuel rod was loaded in four-point bending. Figure 27 shows images before (a) and after (b) bending and breaking. The rod displayed brittle behavior. Figure 28 shows the fracture profile for the fractured segment. As in Tests 191 and 192, the fracture occurred near the center of the rupture region, at the location of maximum oxidation and minimum wall thickness.

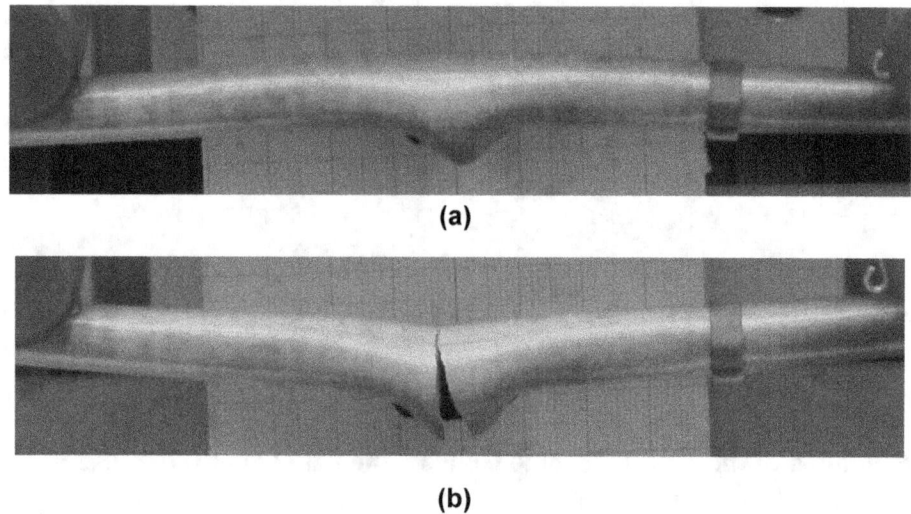

(a)

(b)

Figure 27 Segment 193 (a) before and (b) after four-point bending.

38

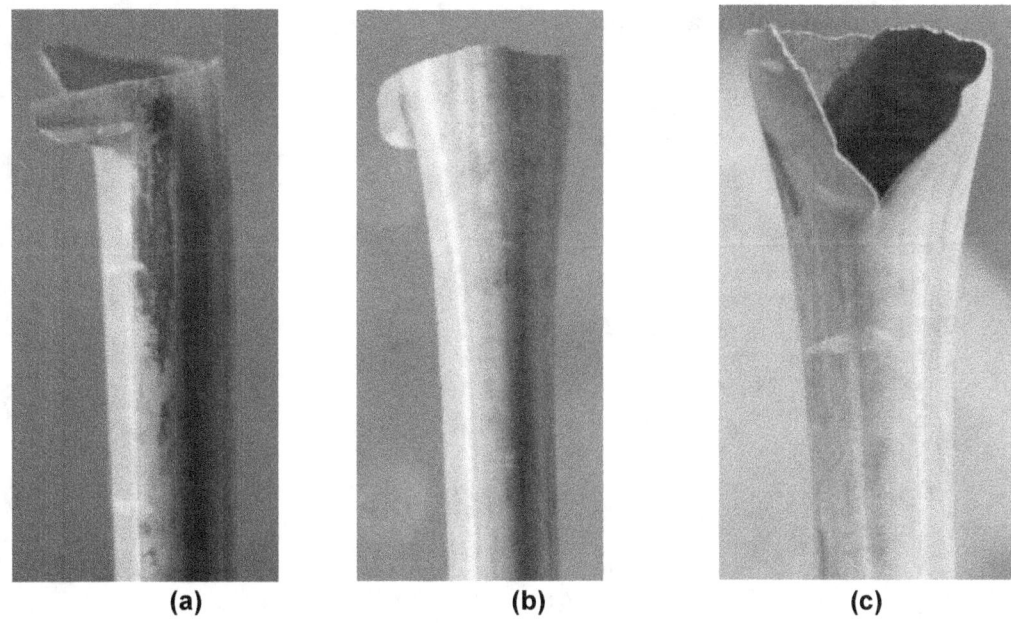

(a)   (b)   (c)

Figure 28 Images of the fracture profile from segment 193 after the four-point bend test of (a) and (b) the bottom half and (c) the top half.

Figure 29 provides the load-displacement curve. The segment withstood a 175-N flexural load before breaking. The x-axis is flexural extension and indicates the displacement of the loading pins. From the load-displacement curve, values of maximum load, failure bending moment, offset displacement at the loading pins, and failure energy were calculated to be 175 N, 4.2 N•m, 0.13 mm, and 0.27 J, respectively.

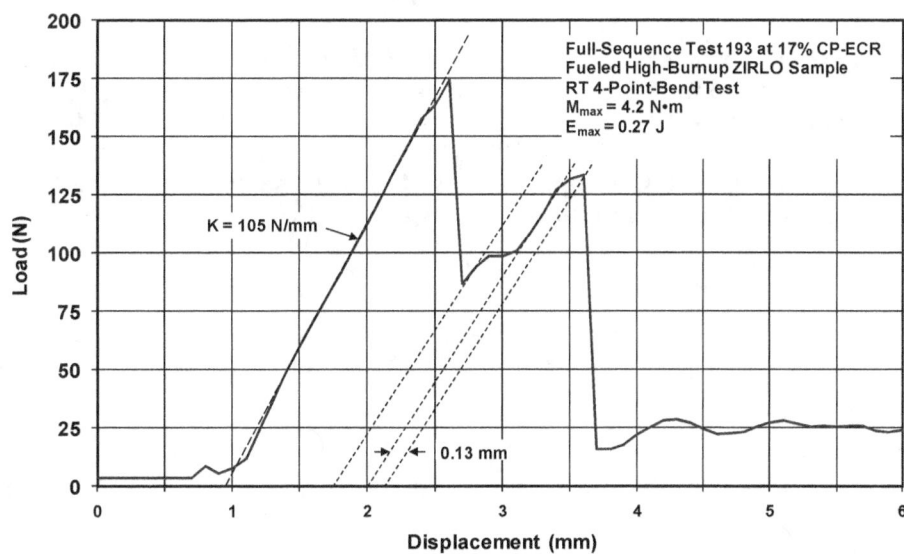

Figure 29 Load-displacement curve for the four-point bend test on segment 193.

39

4.3 Comparison of As-Fabricated and Irradiated Testing Results

The results presented in sections 4.1 and 4.2 for as-fabricated and irradiated testing have been combined and plotted below in Figure 30 and Figure 31.

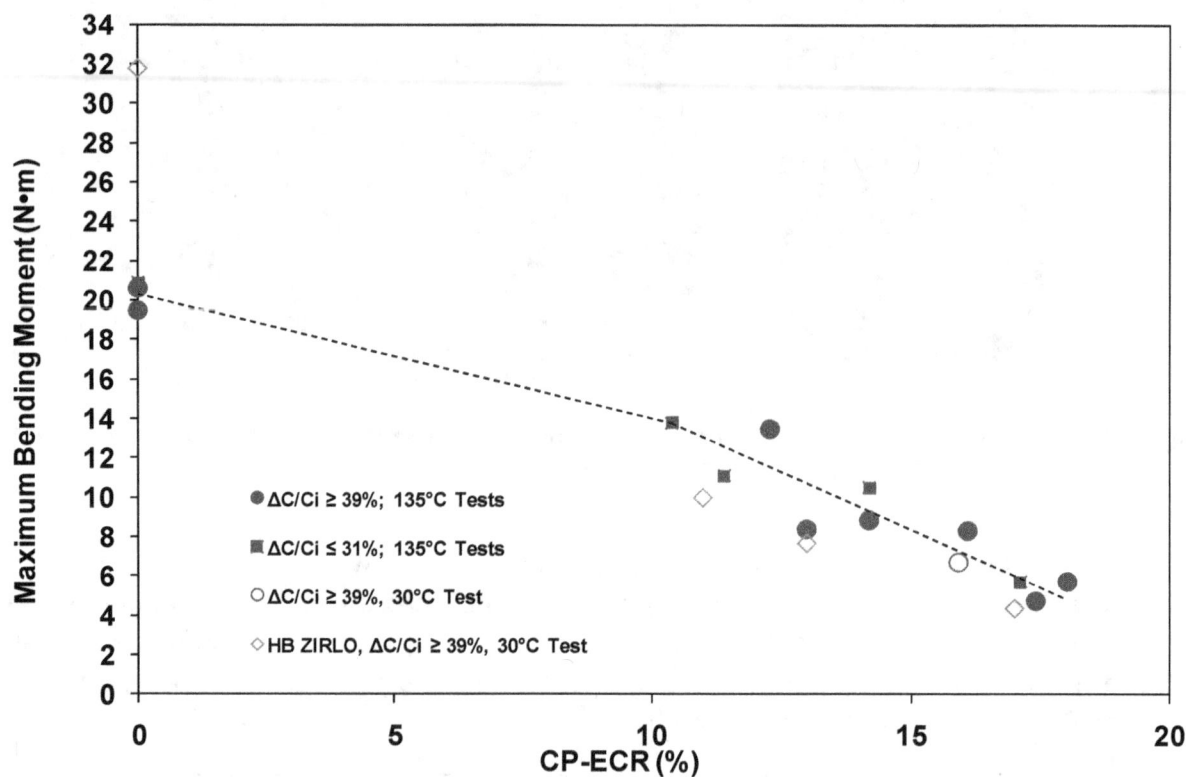

Figure 30 Maximum bending moment as a function of oxidation level for post-LOCA-oxidation samples subjected to four-point bend tests at 1–2 mm/s and either 135 °C or RT (30 °C). For samples at 0% CP-ECR, which did not fail, values are plotted for 14-mm displacement. Argonne data for AF ZIRLO are plotted with blue symbols and Studsvik data for high-burnup ZIRLO samples are plotted with red symbols. The trend line is a best fit to Argonne four-point bend test data at 135 °C.

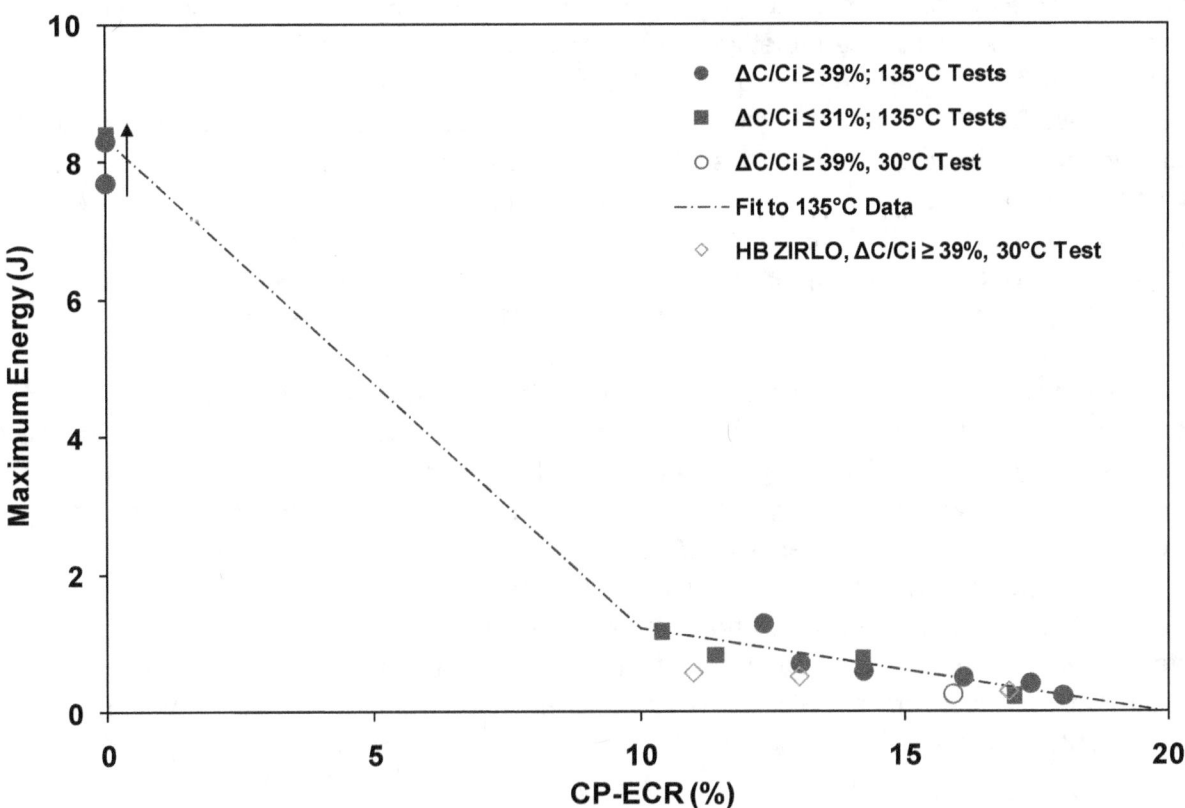

Figure 31 Maximum energy as a function of oxidation level for post-LOCA-oxidation samples subjected to four-point bend tests at 1–2 mm/s and either 135 °C or RT (30 °C). For samples at 0% CP-ECR, which did not fail, maximum energies through 14-mm displacement are plotted. For samples with >10% CP-ECR, data points represent failure energy. Argonne data for AF ZIRLO are plotted with blue symbols and Studsvik data for high-burnup ZIRLO samples are plotted with red symbols. The trend line is a best fit to Argonne four-point bend test data at 135 °C.

The best-fit lines for ANL 135 degrees C 4-PBT data with as-fabricated (AF) ZIRLO cladding samples oxidized to greater than or equal to 10 percent CP-ECR are the following:

$$M_{max} = 13.96 - 1.090 \, (CP\text{-}ECR - 10\%) \tag{1}$$

$$E_{max} = 1.219 - 0.1214 \, (CP\text{-}ECR - 10\%) \tag{2}$$

where M_{max} is in N•m and E_{max} is in J. At 17 percent CP-ECR, the correlations give 6.3 N•m and 0.37 J at 135 degrees C 4-PBT temperature. For the Studsvik 30 degrees C 4-PBTs with high-burnup cladding containing about 200-wppm hydrogen, the average values were 8.5 N•m and 0.54 J at 12±1 percent CP-ECR. The Studsvik 4-PBTs were conducted at RT. ANL did one RT test with AF ZIRLO oxidized to 16 percent CP-ECR. The maximum bending moment (6.7 N•m) and energy (0.26 J) were lower than the Studsvik values at 12±1 percent CP-ECR.

One observation available from evaluating Figure 30 and Figure 31 is that the bending moment for irradiated fuel rods is reduced relative to as-fabricated cladding with the same oxidation level. There are too few data to draw quantitative conclusions; however, some reduction is apparent. Based on LOCA-embrittlement data for high-burnup cladding, the ductile-to-brittle oxidation level for 200-wppm hydrogen is 12 percent. Test samples 191 and 192 had about 200-wppm hydrogen and were oxidized to CP-ECR levels just above and below the 12-percent limit. One purpose of the Studsvik tests was to determine if the maximum bending moment and failure energy were at least as high at the embrittlement limit as the values for AF cladding oxidized to 17 percent CP-ECR. Figure 30 and Figure 31 show that this is the case.

If the impact of hydrogen on the mechanical behavior of ballooned and ruptured cladding was exactly that measured by ring-compression testing of nondeformed cladding samples, it would be expected that the value of bending moment and failure energy for high-burnup cladding containing about 200-wppm hydrogen and oxidized to 12 percent CP-ECR would be exactly that of AF cladding oxidized to 17 percent CP-ECR. There are too few data to draw detailed conclusions on the impact of hydrogen on the mechanical behavior of ballooned and ruptured cladding relative to that measured by ring-compression testing of nondeformed cladding samples. It would require a substantial, well-instrumented testing program to confirm that post-LOCA strength and toughness are preserved for oxidation embrittlement limits based on hydrogen content according to the correlation observed in ring-compression testing.

Examining Figure 30 and Figure 31 suggests that localized oxidation (when calculated with the thinned cladding wall thickness) has a first-order impact on reducing the mechanical behavior of the balloon region, while balloon size and bend-test temperature are lower order variables, or are not variables, in the prediction of maximum bending moment and maximum energy. The data plotted in Figure 30 and Figure 31 are from tests with balloon sizes ranging from 21 percent to 69 percent, and yet there is surprisingly little scatter when the localized oxidation is calculated with the thinned cladding wall thickness.

To say more about the impact of balloon size on the mechanical behavior of ballooned and oxidized cladding, the data in Figure 30 were also evaluated with the calculated CP-ECR in terms of the original cladding wall thickness. As mentioned in section 4, when CP-ECR values are reported for ballooned and ruptured cladding in this report, the values have been determined assuming double-sided oxidation and taking the average wall thickness in the rupture region as the denominator of the CP-ECR equation. When the original cladding wall thickness was used to determine CP-ECR and the data were plotted, the data scatter increased. This suggests that accounting for the effect of balloon size by taking the average wall thickness in the rupture region as the denominator of the CP-ECR equation provides an appropriate normalizing factor.

In addition to localized oxidation, regions of high hydrogen absorption within the ballooned and ruptured region present an additional degradation mechanism to mechanical behavior of ballooned and ruptured cladding. For the oxidized integral tests at Studsvik with ballooning strains near 50 percent, fracture always occurred in the center of the rupture region, where localized oxidation is greatest (in terms of percent cladding reacted) due to wall thinning. For the oxidized integral tests at ANL, with the exception of the OCZL#25 sample, LOCA integral samples with circumferential strains less than or equal to 32 percent failed in a region where the cladding was fully brittle between the rupture tips and the hydrogen peaks (see Section 5.1). Samples with greater than or equal to 40 percent rupture strain failed in the rupture node location where some of the cladding had significant local ductility (e.g., thick backside of the balloon). The bending moments and failure energy of samples that failed in the rupture node or outside of the rupture node are plotted together in Figure 30 and Figure 31; however, no obvious trend is observed to differentiate these two data sets. Even when fracture occurred away from the center of the rupture region, where significant hydrogen absorption took place during high-temperature oxidation, the bending moment and failure energy still are shown to decrease with increasing oxidation consistent with samples that failed in the center of the rupture region. This suggests that limiting oxidation preserves mechanical behavior in the ballooned and ruptured region of a fuel rod, even when additional degradation mechanisms beyond localized oxidation are present.

5. CONCLUSIONS

The purpose of this document is to serve as the technical basis for the treatment of the ballooned and ruptured regions of a fuel rod in LOCA analysis. The technical basis is founded on the results of the NRC's integral LOCA research program, which was designed to measure the mechanical behavior of ballooned and ruptured cladding following LOCA conditions. The results and observations of the integral LOCA program have been used to develop conclusions about the impact of hydrogen and burnup on the mechanical behavior of ballooned and ruptured cladding following LOCA conditions. These conclusions have been used to develop recommendations for regulatory requirements for the treatment of the ballooned and ruptured regions of a fuel rod in LOCA analysis. This section will present the conclusions of the NRC's LOCA research program, along with the development of recommendations based on these conclusions.

5.1 Treatment of the Ballooned Region within the Rulemaking To Revise 10 CFR 50.46(b)

The LOCA acceptance criteria that limit peak oxidation temperature and maximum oxidation level as a function of hydrogen content are based on retention of ductility. Although the criteria may protect the ballooned and ruptured region from severing and fragmenting during and following quench, ductility will not be retained everywhere in this region. Higher hydrogen-content regions from the rupture edge to the hydrogen peak will contain brittle material. Also, within the rupture region cross sections, the cladding transitions from brittle (at the thin, heavily oxidized rupture tips) to ductile (at the thicker back regions that are at lower oxidation levels) at 17 percent oxidation level. Although the rupture node contains material that is locally ductile, it is difficult to observe such ductility in a structural test such as the 4-PBT and to determine non-zero offset displacement from the load-displacement curve.

For unrestrained as-fabricated cladding, quench will induce a sharp thermal gradient across the cladding wall such that the outer surface will be cooler than the inner surface. Both hoop ($(\sigma_\theta)_{th}$)

and axial ($(\sigma_z)_{th}$) thermal stresses are induced in the cladding such that the outer cladding surface is in tension and the inner cladding surface is in compression. Regardless of the magnitude of these stresses, ballooned, ruptured, and oxidized (at 1,200 degrees C) cladding segments tested in the NRC's integral LOCA research program survived quench without failure.

The location of failure within the ballooned and ruptured region under four-point bending was found to occur in either the middle of the rupture node, where local oxidation was greatest, or in a region of high hydrogen content above and/or below the rupture node. The location of failure appeared to be influenced by the balloon size. However, even when fracture occurred away from the center of the rupture region, where significant hydrogen absorption took place during high-temperature oxidation, the bending moment and failure energy were still shown to decrease with increasing oxidation consistent with samples that failed in the center of the rupture region. When the bending moments and failure energy of samples that failed in the rupture node or outside of the rupture node are plotted together, no obvious trend is observed to differentiate these two data sets. This suggests that limiting oxidation preserves mechanical behavior in the ballooned and ruptured region of a fuel rod, even when additional degradation mechanisms beyond localized oxidation are present.

The bending moments (measure of strength) and the failure energies (measure of toughness) measured in the NRC's integral LOCA program exhibited smooth trends toward very low values with increasing oxidation level but remained significantly above zero for oxidation levels less than or equal to 17 percent. Values comparable to those determined for as-fabricated cladding at 17 percent CP-ECR (M_{max} = 6.3 N•m and E_{max} = 0.37 J) were found when oxidation was limited in accordance with RCT results from nondeformed samples containing preoxidation hydrogen. These observations suggest that, when oxidation is limited in accordance with RCT results from nondeformed samples containing preoxidation hydrogen, values comparable to those determined for as-fabricated cladding at 17 percent CP-ECR may be found. Said in another way, restricting the oxidation level in the balloon region based on the results of RCTs from cladding with the same pretransient hydrogen content for high-burnup ballooned and ruptured samples appears to preserve strength and toughness relative to values for as-fabricated cladding oxidized to 17 percent CP-ECR in the ballooned region.

Therefore, the Office of Nuclear Regulatory Research recommendation for how to treat the ballooned region is that the time-at-temperature limit developed based on ring-compression data to limit oxidation is applied uniformly to the entire rod, with the provisions for the balloon outlined in the existing rule to use the average wall thickness in the rupture region to calculate the CP-ECR.

5.2 Extrapolation of Research Findings to New Cladding Alloys and Lower Oxidation Temperatures

One expectation of the NRC's integral LOCA research program was that quantitative conclusions could be made about the degradation with oxidation, burnup, and hydrogen content in the ballooned and ruptured region of a fuel rod, in comparison with that measured with RCTs of nondeformed cladding materials. Particularly, the expectation was that a relationship could be developed between the degradation of mechanical behavior in the balloon region and the degradation of ductility in nondeformed regions, as measured by RCTs. With a particular relationship between degradation of mechanical behavior in the balloon region and degradation of ductility as measured by RCTs, a regulatory requirement could be informed by RCTs alone. Ring-compression testing provides a simple, pass-fail testing approach that uses common tooting equipment and a relatively small sample size and therefore offers an advantage. With a relationship between ring-compression data and degradation in the ballooned and ruptured region of a fuel rod as a function of oxidation, new cladding designs with improved embrittlement performance observed in RCTs or embrittlement limits developed from ring-compression testing at temperatures less than 1,200 degrees C could then be applied in the balloon region in a standard way.

With the limited data, a definitive and quantitative conclusion cannot be stated about the relationship between degradation of mechanical behavior in the balloon region and degradation of ductility as measured by RCTs. This research program only included one cladding alloy, and testing was conducted at a peak cladding temperature of 1,200 degrees C. Therefore, the translation of improved performance in embrittlement behavior seen with some modern alloys, and in tests conducted at lower peak cladding temperatures, to mechanical behavior in the ballooned region is not clear. What can be stated is that the values of bending moment and failure energy have been shown to decrease with increasing oxidation, even through a wide range of values for balloon strain. In addition, even though very high values of hydrogen content were observed surrounding the balloon region for the as-fabricated samples, this did not appear to introduce a separate degradation mechanism that invalidated the observed trend that the values of bending moment and failure energy decreased with increasing oxidation. The results of this program did not reveal any reason that oxidation embrittlement limits developed from RCTs on nondeformed cladding material should not be indicative of trends in the degradation of ballooned and ruptured regions. Said in another way, the results of this program did not reveal any reason that the improved embrittlement performance of new cladding alloys or improved embrittlement performance at lower oxidation temperatures observed in RCTs should not be applied in the balloon region in the manner recommended above.

Different cladding alloys have been shown to exhibit a range of values for yield strength at operating temperatures. Many of these differences in yield strength are attributed to variation in heat treatment, the presence of second-phase precipitates, and other manufacturing variables. Irradiation and hydrogen absorption have also been shown to impact the value of yield strength. Because the findings of this research on the mechanical behavior of the ballooned and ruptured region are related to strength, the impact of the variability of yield strength for different cladding alloys was considered. It was concluded that, because the causes of variability in yield strength at operating temperatures (e.g., second-phase precipitates, heat treatment) are largely annealed out with exposure to the high temperatures of a LOCA, the findings of this research should be relevant to the range of known cladding alloys that exhibit a range of values for yield strength at operating temperatures. This conclusion may need to be revisited if cladding properties and manufacturing variables deviate significantly from modern designs.

In addition, the applicability of the findings of this research on fuel designs with different cladding dimensions was considered. Using the CP-ECR, which is normalized to the cladding thickness, to quantify exposure to high-temperature oxidation means that changes in cladding thickness already impact the calculation. Therefore, it was concluded that the findings of this research should be relevant to the range of known cladding dimensions. This conclusion may need to be revisited if cladding dimensions deviate significantly from modern values.

A more extensive testing program could be conducted that includes (1) alloys with improved as-fabricated embrittlement behavior,[3] (2) testing at lower peak oxidation temperatures, (3) alloys with variability in yield strength at operating temperature, and (4) cladding designs with dimensions other than those tested. Alternatively, mechanical testing of ballooned and ruptured cladding could be required in order to license any embrittlement analytical limits other than that presented in Figure 1. Either of these options may provide greater insight on the performance of ballooned and ruptured regions of fuel rods and particularly insight on the performance of ballooned and ruptured regions when oxidation is limited in accordance with embrittlement limits developed from ring-compression testing.

However, this report has already stated that, in the absence of a credible analysis of loads, cladding stresses, and cladding strains for a degraded LOCA core, there are no absolute metrics to determine how much ductility or strength would be needed to guarantee that fuel-rod cladding would maintain its geometry during and following LOCA quench. Without a specific and quantified requirement for the load, cladding stress, and cladding strain that cladding must survive without failure, or without an analysis that defines the extent of cladding failure that can be experienced before challenging core coolability, the value of a more refined characterization of the mechanical behavior of ballooned and ruptured cladding is not clear. Therefore, pursuing a more extensive testing program or requiring further testing of ballooned and ruptured cladding in order to license any embrittlement analytical limits other than that presented in Figure 1 is not recommended at this time.

5.3 Alternate Performance Metrics for the Ballooned and Ruptured Region of a Fuel Rod

The limited data from the integral testing of high-burnup materials in the NRC's integral LOCA research program is not sufficient for developing a separate performance metric for the ballooned and ruptured region of a fuel rod. The findings of this research are limited to the conclusion that restricting the oxidation level in the balloon region provides for the retention of mechanical behavior (quench survival and residual ability to survive some amount of loading). Further, restricting the oxidation level in the balloon region of high-burnup fuel rods based on the pretransient hydrogen content appears to preserve strength and toughness relative to values for as-fabricated cladding oxidized to 17 percent CP-ECR in the ballooned region.

---

[3] In the NRC's LOCA research program, some modern alloys exhibited improved embrittlement performance when tested in the as-fabricated conditions. As the alloy hydrogen content was increased, this improvement largely diminished.

Within the international community, there has been longstanding discussion of alternate metrics for fuel rod performance under LOCA conditions. Proposals include defining an acceptable strength threshold and then using experimental data to set limits for oxidation that have been shown to preserve that level of strength. Alternatively, an acceptable degree of fracture toughness could be defined and experimental data could be used to set limits for oxidation that have been shown to preserve that level of fracture toughness. Others have proposed looking for a criterion that is more mechanistically related to mechanical degradation than calculated ECR, such as oxygen content in the residual beta layer of the cladding material.

As stated above, in the absence of a credible analysis of loads, cladding stresses, and cladding strains for a degraded LOCA core, there are no absolute metrics to determine how much ductility, fracture toughness, or strength would be needed to guarantee that fuel-rod cladding would maintain its geometry during and following LOCA quench. It is also not clear what impact the severing of some fuel rods into two pieces would have on core coolability. Without a specific and quantified requirement for the load, cladding stress, and cladding strain that cladding must survive without failure, or without an analysis that defines the extent of cladding failure that can be experienced before challenging core coolability, the ability to define a separate performance metric for the ballooned and ruptured region of a fuel rod is not clear.

Regarding the development of a performance metric more mechanistically related to mechanical degradation than calculated ECR, such as oxygen content or thickness of the residual beta layer of the cladding material, it is clear this would be advantageous and useful. However, developing models to predict the oxygen content and oxygen diffusion is complex, and integrating those models into LOCA analysis has proven difficult. The current state of the art in modeling has not advanced to a point where this approach is practical for LOCA analysis. Particularly when considering the balloon region, this analysis approach would require more precise knowledge of ballooning strain values and improved predictive capabilities. Calculated ECR is a simple and straightforward calculation that has been shown to be correlated with mechanical performance of fuel and cladding materials. There are alternative metrics that arguably offer a more mechanistic approach than the one that is recommended here; however, the state of the art makes developing regulations and implementing these metrics in analysis space based in these metrics difficult. Therefore, pursuing alternative performance metrics, particularly for ballooned and ruptured regions, is not recommended at this time.

5.4 Summary of Conclusions

In summary, the following are the conclusions of the integral LOCA program:

- Bending moment and failure energy can be measured using the 4-PBT to determine the resistance to fracturing of ballooned cladding during a LOCA.

- The values of bending moment and failure energy have been shown to decrease with increasing oxidation, even through a wide range of values for balloon strain.

- Even though very high values of hydrogen content were observed after oxidation within the balloon region for the as-fabricated samples, this did not appear to introduce a separate degradation mechanism that invalidated the observed trend that the values of bending moment and failure energy decreased with increasing oxidation.

- The values of bending moment and failure energy for irradiated fuel rods have been shown to be reduced relative to as-fabricated cladding with the same oxidation level.

- Limiting oxidation in the ballooned and ruptured region is appropriate, and the limit should be reduced from 17 percent for high-burnup cladding

- Values comparable to those determined for as-fabricated cladding at 17 percent CP-ECR may be found when oxidation is limited in accordance with the reduced, hydrogen-based oxidation limit.

- Said another way, restricting the oxidation level based on the pretransient hydrogen content for high-burnup ballooned and ruptured samples appears to preserve strength and toughness relative to values for as-fabricated cladding oxidized to 17 percent CP-ECR in the ballooned region.

- The results of this program did not reveal any reason that new cladding designs with improved embrittlement performance observed in RCTs, or embrittlement limits developed from ring-compression testing at temperatures less than 1,200 degrees C, should not be applied in the balloon region in the manner recommended above.

- The research program was not extensive enough to develop any alternate metric, and pursuing an alternate metric, particularly for the ballooned and ruptured region of a fuel rod, is not recommended at this time.

6. RECOMMENDATIONS

For the purposes of rulemaking to revise 10 CFR 50.46(b), the Office of Nuclear Regulatory Research recommends that the time-at-temperature limit derived from ring-compression data to limit oxidation be applied uniformly to the entire rod, including the ballooned region. As is outlined in the current rule, the average wall thickness in the rupture region should be used to calculate the CP-ECR to account for ballooning.

7. REFERENCES

1. *U. S. Code of Federal Regulations*, "Domestic Licensing of Production and Utilization Facilities," Part 50, Chapter I, Title 10, "Energy."

2. Opinion of the Commission. Atomic Energy Commission Rule-Making Hearing. RM-50-1, December 28, 1973.

3. U.S. Nuclear Regulatory Commission, "Technical Basis for Revision of Embrittlement Criteria in 10 CFR 50.46," Research Information Letter 0801, May 30, 2008, Agencywide Documents Access and Management System (ADAMS) Accession No. ML081350225.

4. U.S. Nuclear Regulatory Commission, "Cladding Embrittlement during Postulated Loss-Of-Coolant Accidents," NUREG/CR-6967, July 2008, ADAMS Accession No. ML082130389.

5. Yan, Y., T.A. Burtseva, and M.C. Billone, Argonne National Laboratory letter report to U.S. Nuclear Regulatory Commission, "Post-Quench Ductility Results for North Anna High-Burnup 17×17 ZIRLO Cladding with Intermediate Hydrogen Content," April 17, 2009, ADAMS Accession No. ML091200702.

6. Billone, M., Argonne National Laboratory letter report to U.S. Nuclear Regulatory Commission, "Cladding Tests for LOCA Conditions, Monthly Letter Status Report for June 2009 for JCN N6684," October 22, 2009. ADAMS Accession No. ML113610558.

7. Hache, G., and H.M. Chung, "The History of LOCA Embrittlement Criteria," NEA/CSNI/R(2001)18, Nuclear Energy Agency, Committee on the Safety of Nuclear Installations, Aix-en-Provence, France, March 2001.

8. Nuclear Energy Agency, Organisation for Economic Co-Operation and Development, "Nuclear Fuel Behavior in Loss-of-Coolant Accident (LOCA) Conditions, State-of–the-Art Report," NEA No. 6846, 2009.

9. Billone, M., "Assessment of Current Test Methods for Post-LOCA Cladding Behavior," Argonne National Laboratory, March 2011. ADAMS Accession No. ML113640254.

10. Nuclear Energy Agency, Organization for Economic Co-Operation and Development, "LOCA Fuel Cladding Test Methodologies, Compilation of Responses and Recommended Test Characteristics Technical Note," NEA/SEN/SIN/FUEL(2007)2

11. Nuclear Energy Agency, Organization for Economic Co-Operation and Development, "Review of High Burnup RIA and LOCA Database and Criteria," NEA/CSNI/R(2006)5

12. Nuclear Energy Agency, Organization for Economic Co-Operation and Development, "LOCA Criteria Basis and Test Methodology" CSNI Technical Opinion Paper No. 13, NEA No. NEA/CSNI/R(2011)7

13. Brachet, J.-C., V. Vandenberghe-Maillot, L. Portier, D. Gilbon, A. Lesbros, N. Waeckel, and J.-P. Mardon, "Hydrogen Content, Preoxidation, and Cooling Scenario Effects on Post-Quench Microstructure and Mechanical Properties of Zircaloy-4 and M5® Alloys in LOCA Conditions," *Journal of ASTM International*, Vol. 5, Issue 5 (2008).

14. Vandenberghe, V., J.C. Brachet, M. Le Saux, D. Gilbon, M. Billone, D. Hamon, J.P. Mardon, and H. Hafidi, "Influence of the Cooling Scenario on the Post-Quench Mechanical Properties of Pre-Hydrided Zircaloy-4 Fuel Claddings after High Temperature Steam Oxidation (LOCA Conditions)," Orlando, FL: LWR Fuel Performance/TopFuel/WRFPM , September 26–29, 2010, Paper 096.

15. Billone, M., "Analysis of Data from Studsvik LOCA with High-Burnup ZIRLO," Letter Report, Argonne National Laboratory, March 2011. ADAMS Accession No. ML113640255.

16. Nagase, F., and T. Fuketa, "Effect of Pre-Hydriding on Thermal Shock Resistance of Zircaloy-4 Cladding under Simulated Loss-of-Coolant Accident Conditions," *Journal of Nuclear Science and Technology*, 41:723–730 (2004).

17. USNRC staff report, "Fuel Fragmentation, Relocation and Dispersal during the Loss-of-Coolant Accident," Draft completed July 2011, to be published

18. Nagase, F., and T. Fuketa, "Behavior of Pre-Hydrided Zircaloy-4 Cladding under Simulated LOCA Conditions," *Journal of Nuclear Science and Technology*, 42:209–218. (2005)

19. Nagase, F., and T. Fuketa, "Fracture Behavior of Irradiated Zircaloy-4 Cladding under Simulated LOCA Conditions," *Journal of Nuclear Science and Technology*, 43:1114-1119. (2006)

20. Nagase, F., T. Chuto, and T. Fuketa, "Behavior of High Burn-up Fuel Cladding under LOCA Conditions," *Journal of Nuclear Science and Technology*, 46:763–769. (2009)

21. Yan, Y., T.A. Burtseva, R.O. Meyer, and M.C. Billone, Argonne National Laboratory letter report to U.S. Nuclear Regulatory Commission, "Update of LOCA-Integral and Post-LOCA-Bend Test Results for Fresh ZIRLO Cladding," July 21, 2010. ADAMS Accession No. ML111380437.

22. Argonne National Laboratory letter report to U.S. Nuclear Regulatory Commission, "Argonne Results for ANL-Studsvik Benchmark Tests," August 13, 2010. ADAMS Accession No. ML111380445.

APPENDIX A

Discussion of the Typicality of Test Conditions in Integral Loss-of-Coolant Accident Tests at Argonne National Laboratory and Studsvik

The integral loss-of-coolant accident (LOCA) tests conducted at Argonne National Laboratory (ANL) and Studsvik were designed to develop understanding of the impact of LOCA conditions on the mechanical behavior of ballooned and ruptured fuel rods. A test train and experiment design were developed that could generate data for this purpose. There are aspects of the test train and experiment design that are typical of conditions expected in a reactor during a LOCA, and there are aspects that are not typical. This appendix will discuss the test train and experimental design in comparison to expected in-reactor conditions for the purpose of understanding the applicability of the data generated in these experiments.

Characteristics of Test Train: Rod Length, Axial Constraint, and Heat Source

The fuel rod segments used for the integral LOCA tests were 300 millimeters (mm) in length (about 1 foot (ft)) (full-length fuel rods are about 12 ft long). At both ANL and Studsvik laboratories, the test train accommodates a single fuel rod segment within a quartz tube about 2 inches in diameter. One consequence of this single-rod design is that it permits significant expansion during ballooning as well as the possibility of bowing of the test segment during the test. In a fuel assembly, each fuel rod will have far less room to expand or bow before making contact with a neighboring rod. The test train was designed to permit free expansion of the test segment in the axial direction in order to avoid the development of axial constraint or loading when the test segment experiences thermal expansion. However, in a reactor during a LOCA, axial constraint and loading is predicted to occur.

In a reactor, the heat source during a LOCA would be the fuel within the cladding, and therefore the external heating provided by this test train may introduce differences from in-reactor conditions. For one, the fuel in these tests will only reach the maximum furnace temperature (as accommodated by the thermal conductivity of the cladding, fill gas, and fuel); in a reactor, the fuel will reach temperatures higher than the cladding. This difference would have an impact on the pellet expansion behavior as well as the rod gas expansion, although it is not clear if the impact would lead to significantly different ballooning behavior.

Rod Internal Pressure and Ballooning Conditions: Rod Fill Pressure and Gas Void Volume

The tests conducted at ANL on as-fabricated 17×17 ZIRLO cladding filled with zirconia pellets were pressurized to 400–1,600 pounds per square inch, gauge (psig) to induce ballooning strains of varying size. For the tests conducted at Studsvik on irradiated, high-burnup fuel rods, ballooning strain was not an intended variable. The target balloon size for tests at Studsvik was 40 percent balloon strain, and the values of rod internal pressure for the irradiated testing were chosen in order to induce this balloon strain.

For as-fabricated cladding, the rod internal pressure that generated ballooning strains around 40 percent was 1,200 psig. Therefore, testing at Studsvik began with values of rod internal pressure of 1,600 psig to account for the effect of irradiation and hydrogen. A rod internal pressure of 1,600 psig is on the high end of best-estimate rod internal pressure values for a typical reactor core.

For Tests 192 and 193, the rod internal pressure was reduced to 1,200 pounds per square inch (psi). This was done because the comparison between rupture characteristics of fresh material and irradiated material did not indicate the expected impact of irradiation and hydrogen content. In addition, the dimensions of the rupture openings seen in both Tests 189 and 191 were larger than expected for in-reactor rupture openings.

The void volume in both the ANL and Studsvik test segment designs is less than 10 cubic centimeters. Minimizing the void volume was an objective in the test train and rodlet fabrication design. Ten cubic centimeters was determined to be the minimum void volume achievable experimentally. This volume is smaller than the total volume in full-length rods and greater than a volume scaled simply by the segment axial length. Vendors vary their as-fabricated void volume and fill pressure based on experience with their fuel. Some fuels have about 1 percent fission gas release, while others have as much as 15 percent fission gas release. Also, fill pressure and void volume may vary within a single core; therefore, defining "typical" void volume is difficult.

The void volume in these tests is located in three void regions: the pressure fill line, the segment top plenum, and the segment bottom plenum. All of these regions are outside of the central region heated by the furnace and therefore are at a temperature less than the thermocouple readings. The ballooning and rupture typically takes place near the center of the segment length, and therefore the void volume could be considered to be about 150 mm away from the rupture location. The total void volume and distance between the void volume and rupture location are important because discussions surrounding the Halden LOCA tests[4] have pointed to these characteristics as providing for relatively more gas (as compared to full-length rods) to drive ballooning, fuel relocation, and expulsion. The distance between the void volume and the peak temperature location in an in-reactor LOCA transient is probably greater than the distance between the experimental void volume and the peak power location—depending on the nature of the transient (i.e., calculations of some small-break LOCA transients predict ballooning and rupture near the top of the fuel rod and therefore not far from the plenum void volume).

The Nuclear Energy Agency Committee on the Safety of Nuclear Installations recently (November 2010) issued a report, "Safety Significance of the Halden IFA-650 LOCA Test Results" (see http://www.oecd-nea.org/nsd/docs/2010/csni-r2010-5.pdf), in which the effect of gas flow was discussed. This well-articulated and thorough discussion is mentioned here because many of the statements are directly relevant to the ANL and Studsvik tests. The void volume in the tests at ANL and Studsvik is smaller than in the Halden test setup, but the distance between the void volume and the peak temperature location is similar for the two programs. The discussion about gas flow in the Halden report suggested a strong correlation between the characteristics of gas flow (total volume, distance, and gas flow blockage due to fuel cladding bonding) and the ejection of fuel from the test segment.

---

[4] The void volume in Halden's test setup is about 17 cubic centimeters.

Temperature Transient: Heatup Rate, Maximum Temperature, and Quench Conditions

The temperature transient programmed for the integral tests at ANL and Studsvik is comparable in heatup rate, cooldown rate, and quench temperature to that used throughout the NRC's LOCA program at ANL. The cladding was heated at 5 degrees Celsius (C) per second (s) to 1,200 degrees C in steam, held at 1,200 degrees C, cooled at 3 degrees C/s to 800 degrees C, and rapidly cooled via water quench from 800 degrees C to 100 degrees C. The hold time at the peak cladding temperature was changed between tests in order to control the total oxidation level as calculated by the Cathcart-Pawel equation for the equivalent cladding reacted (CP-ECR). The heatup and cooldown rates, as well as the quench temperature, are considered to be representative of large-break LOCA conditions. The peak temperature for most tests was at the regulatory limit for cladding peak temperature during a LOCA. The exceptions were the ramp-to-rupture tests, which were terminated just after rupture occurred. For these tests, the peak temperature was well below the regulatory limit.

As mentioned previously, the fuel temperature was limited by the external heating and is expected to be lower than the fuel temperature in realistic LOCA conditions.

APPENDIX B

Benchmarking Argonne National Laboratory and Studsvik Bend Equipment

Irradiated, high-burnup cladding material was tested at Studsvik. Benchmarking and characterization tests were conducted at Studsvik with as-received cladding material in order to validate the test device and procedures, as well as to confirm that the results of tests at Studsvik were directly comparable to results from parallel tests at Argonne National Laboratory (ANL).

ANL conducted a room temperature (RT) four-point bend test (4-PBT) with an as-fabricated (AF) ZIRLO^{TM} sample received in 2003. It is not the same lot of ZIRLO used in the Studsvik benchmark; however, it is still useful to compare results. The net sample displacement for the ANL test was 13.73 millimeters (mm). The Studsvik benchmark data were truncated at a net sample displacement of 13.79 mm, which is close enough for comparison. The results are summarized in Table and in Figure (ANL) and Figure (Studsvik). Differences in the results are relatively small and within variation from one lot of ZIRLO to another. The comparison confirms that the 4-PBT results are consistent.

There is a difference in length (L_s) between the supports of the 4-PBT fixtures: 250 mm for ANL and 246.4 mm for Studsvik. This difference in L_s results is a difference in calculated loading stiffness (K = [0.8064 newton (N)/mm^5] I for ANL and K = [0.8734 N/mm^5] I for Studsvik, where the area moment of inertia I is related to outer and inner radii by $I = [\pi/4] [R_o^4 - R_i^4]$) and the relationship between maximum bending moment and maximum load is (M_{max} = 0.025-meter (m) P_{max} for ANL and M_{max} = 0.0241-m P_{max} for Studsvik). These differences are reflected in the values given in Table .

Table B-1 Comparison of Argonne National Laboratory and Studsvik Four-Point Bend Test Results at RT and 1 mm/s Displacement Rate at the Loading Points. Argonne Sample: 9.47-mm Outer Diameter, 0.58-mm Wall Thickness, and 165-mm^4 Area Moment of Inertia. Studsvik Sample: 9.50-mm Outer Diameter, 0. 56-mm Wall Thickness, and 158-mm^4 Area Moment of Inertia.

4-PBT	Calculated K, N/mm	Measured K, N/mm	M_{max}, N•m	E_{max}, J	Offset Displacement, mm
Argonne	133	135	33.9	11.3	3.6
Studsvik	138	149	36.1	12.6	3.7

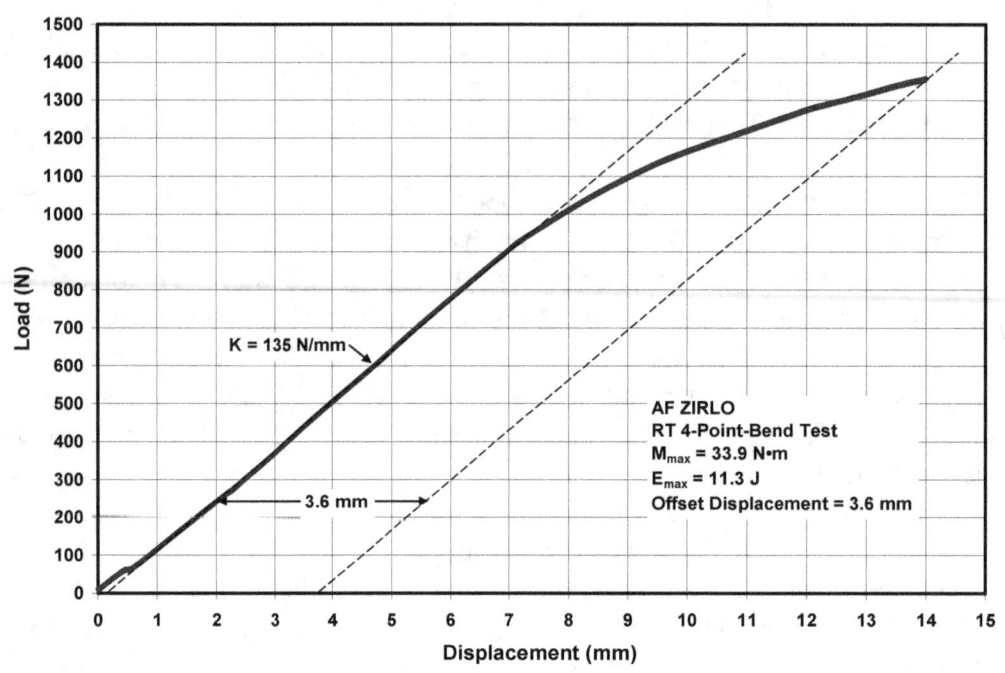

Figure B-1 Load-displacement curve for Argonne National Laboratory four-point bend test benchmark conducted with AF ZIRLO-2003 at RT and 1 mm/s.

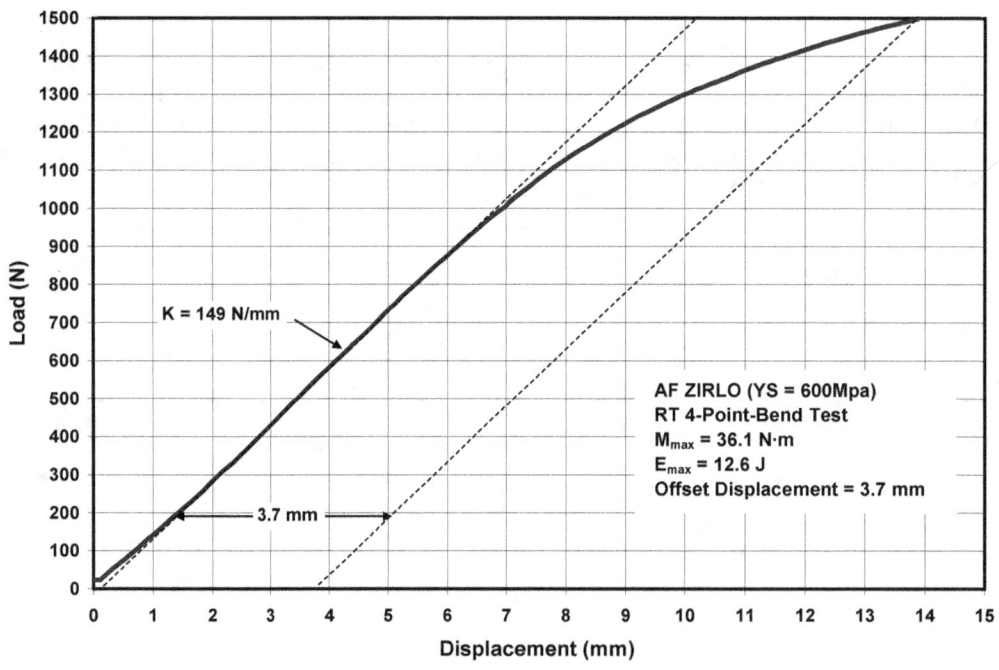

Figure B-2 Load-displacement curve for Studsvik four-point bend test benchmark conducted with AF ZIRLO at RT and 1 mm/s.

APPENDIX C

Discussion of Results from Other Integral Loss-of-Coolant Accident Test Programs, and Comparison to Four-Point Bend Test Results

To produce ballooned specimens for tensile and bend tests, Argonne National Laboratory (ANL) and the Japan Atomic Energy Agency (JAEA) at its Tokai research center performed loss-of-coolant accident (LOCA) integral experiments with lengths of as-fabricated cladding alloys. In addition, JAEA conducted experiments with prehydrided cladding (Refs. 16, 18) and defueled cladding sectioned from irradiated rods (Refs. 19, 20).

JAEA integral experiments differ from ANL's in terms of sample length, internal pressure and volume, heating rate, hold temperature, cooling rate, and quench temperature. Experimental parameters are compared in Table . (Not included in Table are JAEA specimens with high-burnup Zircaloy-2, ZIRLO^{TM}, MDA, and NDA (Ref. 20).) However, the most significant difference between ANL and JAEA testing has to do with mechanical test methods. ANL performed postquench four-point bend tests (4-PBTs) at 135 degrees Celsius (C), while JAEA performed full and partial axial-restraint tests during cooling from the hold temperature to less than 100 degrees C. The next two sections review the axial tensile tests performed by JAEA and their comparison to the LOCA tests conducted in the NRC's integral LOCA program.

Table C-1 Comparison of ANL (Ref. 21, 22) and JAEA (Ref. 16, 18-20) LOCA Integral Sample and Experimental Parameters. "AF" Is As-Fabricated, "PH" Is Prehydrided, "Irr" Is Irradiated

Parameters	ANL		JAEA		
	AF	PH	AF	PH	Irr
17×17 Cladding	ZIRLO	ZIRLO	Zry-4	Zry-4	Zry-4
Clad OD, mm	9.50	9.50	9.42	9.42	---
Wall Thick., mm	0.57	0.57	0.51	0.51	---
Sample Length, mm (minus end caps)	295	295	570	570	180
Hydrogen Content, wppm	≈10	200–700	≈10	100–1,400	150±40
Pellets	zirconia	zirconia	alumina	alumina	alumina
Pellet Stack Length, mm	280	280	550	550	170
Gas Volume, cm^3	10	10	4.4	4.4	2.4
Internal Pressure, MPa (Gauge)	4.14–8.28 @300 °C	4.14–8.28 @300 °C	5 @ RT	5 @ RT	5 @ RT
Heating Rate, °C/s	5	5	10	10	10
Rupture Temp., °C	843±6 750±7	742 700±30	---	656–880	786±25
Rupture Strain, %	22±3 46±4	57 60±10	35 (avg.)	11–40	16±8
Hold Temp., °C	1,200	1,200	947–1,257	947–1,257	1,030–1,178
Cooling Rate to Quench Temp., °C/s	3	3	20 to 900 °C 5 to 700 °C	20 to 900 °C 5 to 700 °C	20 to 900 °C 5 to 700 °C
Quench Temp., °C	800	800	700	700	700

Axial Tensile Tests Performed by Japan Atomic Energy Agency

Axial tensile tests could be performed on LOCA integral samples, and pulling the sample to failure would give an accurate measure of failure load, as every cross section is exposed to the same tensile load. The measured loads are LOCA-relevant; however, the failure loads are the only meaningful data that could be derived from axial tensile tests. If the load-displacement curve exhibited any offset displacement, it would not be clear whether plastic displacement had occurred within the ruptured region of the balloon, just above and below this region where the temperature drops, or outside the middle region where the cladding is annealed and lightly oxidized with negligible hydrogen pickup. Therefore, plastic displacement (ductility) and failure energy (area under the load-displacement curve) in the balloon region cannot be determined from these tests.

Rather than pulling the sample to failure, the JAEA LOCA integral samples were restrained from axial contraction during the quench in the integral experiment. Both full and partial axial-restraint tests were conducted during cooling from the oxidation temperature to less than 100 degrees C. Figure a shows the gripping mechanism used to restrain the cladding. Figure b shows typical axial load versus time results for fully restrained and partially restrained cases that were limited to maximum axial loads of 735 newtons (N), 540 N (reference JAEA case), and 390 N.

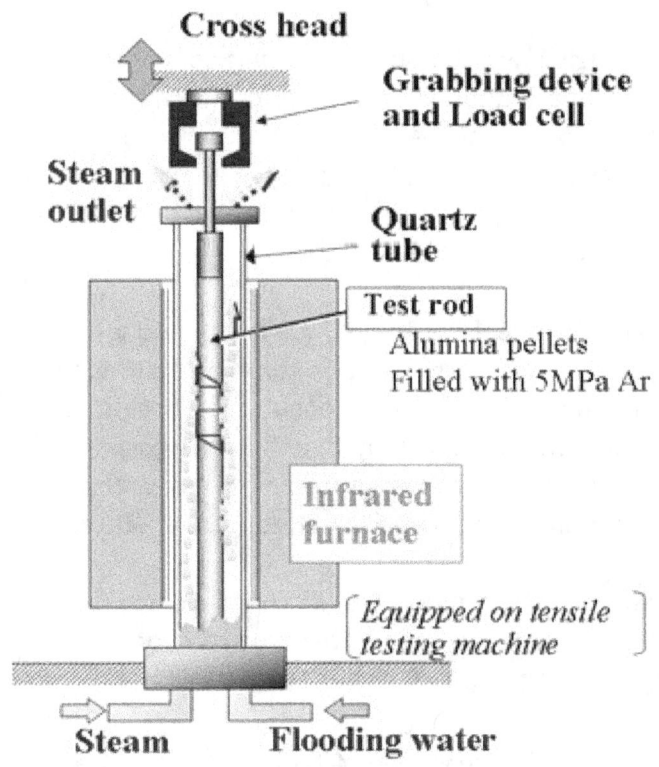

(a) JAEA LOCA apparatus

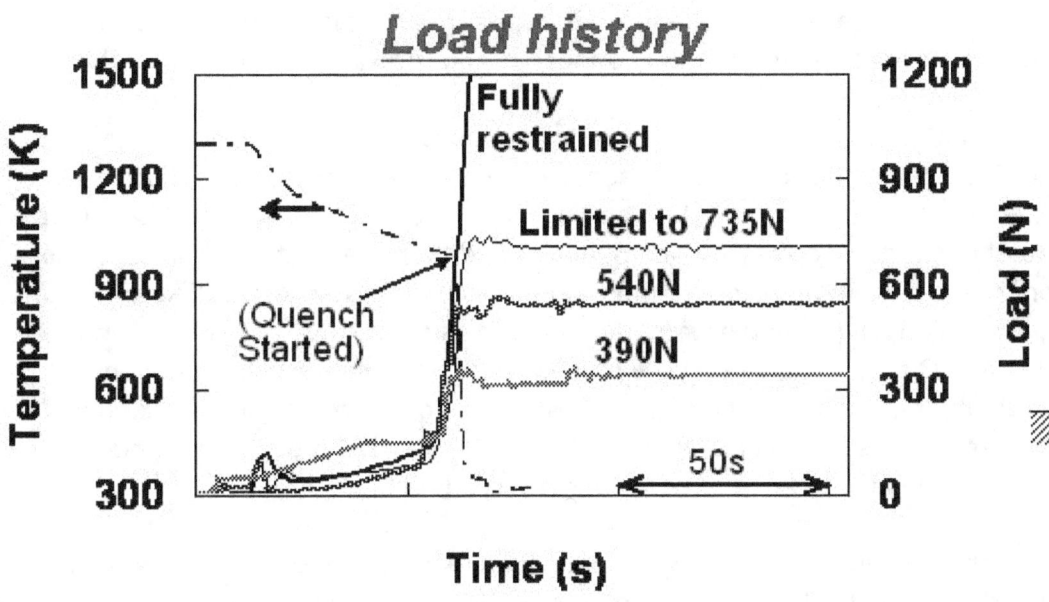

(b) Axial tensile loads vs. time for several constraint conditions

Figure C-2 JAEA LOCA apparatus (a) showing the gripping device used to restrain the sample during cooling and (b) load versus time curves for fully restrained samples and partially restrained (maximum loads of 735 N, 540 N, and 390 N) samples (18).

The measured load is relatively low in these tests during cooling from the oxidation hold temperature to the 700 degrees C quench temperature due to the transition from a bent sample to a straight sample and due to the low yield strength and high plasticity of the cladding metal at elevated temperatures. However, the load builds up rapidly during quench cooling because the metal yield strength increases with decreasing temperature and the metal does not have time to flow plastically to relax the thermal stresses.

For the fully restrained cases (Refs. 16, 18), the maximum load was 1,200 to 2,400 N for samples that survived quench without failure. For samples that failed during quench, the failure loads were 200 to 1,700 N. Most of the failures occurred in the rupture node, which is not expected to pick up additional hydrogen during the oxidation phase. However, these are important results because, regardless of the degree of restraint, the maximum axial load due to differential contraction was found to be less than or equal to 2,400 N.

JAEA conducted 118 tests with prehydrided cladding, which included variation of the hydrogen content, oxidation hold temperature, oxidation hold time, and degree of axial constraint. Forty-seven samples failed during quench, with 42 of the failures occurring in the rupture node.

JAEA also conducted six tests using irradiated Zircaloy-4 (Zry-4) cladding from pressurized-water reactor fuel rods with less than or equal to 44 gigawatt-days per metric ton of uranium burnup, less than or equal to 25-micrometer (μm) corrosion layer, and estimated hydrogen contents in the range of 150±40 weight parts per million (wppm). Based on several analyses of the strength of grid spacers, JAEA argued that axial restraint loads had to be less than 1,000 N. It adopted 540 N for its partially restrained tests using irradiated cladding samples.

For irradiated cladding, the sample length was reduced from 580 millimeters (mm) to 190 mm. Notice in Table 5 that the room temperature (RT) gas volume was reduced from 4.4 cubic centimeters (cm^3) to 2.4 cm^3. Rupture strains were smaller (16±8 percent) than measured for longer, prehydrided test samples of comparable hydrogen content. The smaller gas volume and the shorter (about 40 mm) uniform temperature zone may have contributed to the lower rupture strains. Oxidation temperatures were 1,171±9 degrees C for five of the tests and 1,030 degrees C for one of the tests. Partially restrained tensile tests were conducted during cooling with the maximum axial load set at 540 N. Two of the samples oxidized at about 1,170 degrees C failed at axial loads of 498 N (170 wppm hydrogen and 23 percent CP-ECR) and 385 N (120 wppm hydrogen and 20 percent CP-ECR).

For the sample that fractured at 498 N, posttest imaging (see Figure , taken from Figure 5 in Ref. 19) indicated that failure occurred near the edge of the rupture opening. JAEA interpreted this as a rupture-node failure. However, the results are open to interpretation. In particular, the high hydrogen concentrations near the fracture are indicative of regions outside the rupture opening, which have high hydrogen pickup from inner-surface oxidation. Consistent with JAEA interpretation, the crack may have initiated at the edge of the rupture opening, but it clearly propagated into the high-hydrogen zone outside the rupture opening.

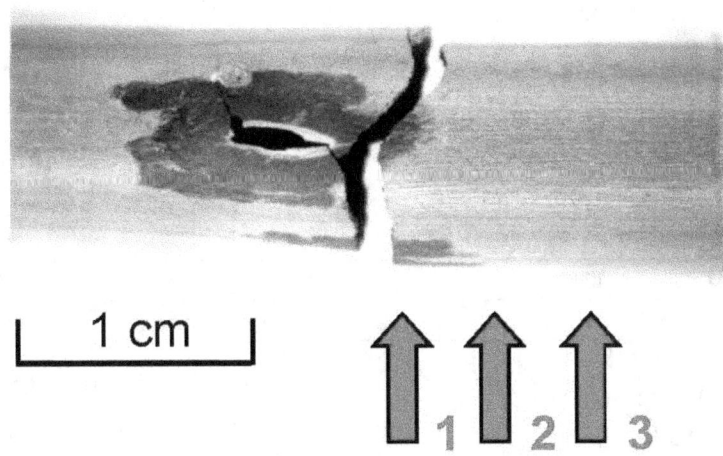

Hydrogen concentration
1. 1450 ppm
2. 1850 ppm
3. 840 ppm

Figure C-3 Appearance of JAEA A 3-1 sample with about 170-wppm pretest hydrogen, oxidized at 1,176 °C to 29.3% BJ-ECR (23% CP-ECR), and partially constrained during cooling to a maximum axial tensile load of 540 N. Measured failure load was 498 N (20).

For nonirradiated cladding, the hydrogen peaks were 30 to 50 mm from the rupture midspan. Based on the results shown in Figure , one hydrogen peak appears to occur at less than 10 mm from the rupture midspan for irradiated Zry-4. It is not clear whether this is due to a difference between irradiated and prehydrided cladding or differences in sample length (190 mm versus 580 mm), uniform temperature zone (40 mm versus 100 mm), and/or rupture strain (14 percent versus 20–40 percent).

Evaluation and Comparison of Loads in Four-Point Loading and Axial Tensile Loading

Four-point bend results can be compared to axial-restraint results, as both tests induce axial stresses. The stress distributions are different, in that the stress acting on a cross section is tensile everywhere in the axial tensile test, while the stress in the axial bend tests varies from tensile to compressive across the cross section. However, failure of a brittle material is governed by the maximum tensile stress. Given the failure bending moment for a 4-PBT, the equivalent axial force that gives the maximum tensile stress can be determined. This determination can be made more easily for a 4-PBT sample that fails outside the rupture region. Figure 6c of the main report shows the severed cross section for the 17 percent CP-ECR sample from Test OCZL#19. The cross section is nearly circular. Table gives the dimensions determined from profilometry, low-magnification metallography, and high-magnification metallography.

Table C-2 Dimensions, Properties, and Failure Bending Moment at Severed Location for Test Sample OCZL#19 with 17% Maximum CP-ECR in the Rupture Node and 12% CP-ECR at the Severed Location.

Parameter	Value	Comment
Outer Diameter (OD, D_o), mm	10.67	Measured
OD Oxide Thickness $(\delta_{ox})_o$, µm	50±6	Measured
Metal OD (D_{mo}), mm	10.57	$D_{mo} = D_o - 2\,(\delta_{ox})_o$
Metal Wall Thickness (h_m), mm	0.46±0.04	Measured
Metal ID (D_{mi}), mm	9.65	$D_{mi} = D_{mo} - 2\,h_m$
ID Oxide Thickness $(\delta_{ox})_i$, µm	35±6	Measured
Inner Diameter (ID, D_i), mm	9.58	$D_i = D_{mi} - 2\,(\delta_{ox})_i$
Cross-sectional Area (A), mm^2		
OD Oxide $(A_{ox})_o$	1.67	$(A_{ox})_o = (\pi/4)\,[(D_o)^2 - (D_{mo})^2]$
Metal (A_m)	14.61	$A_m = (\pi/4)\,[(D_{mo})^2 - (D_{mi})^2]$
ID Oxide $(A_{ox})_i$	1.06	$(A_{ox})_i = (\pi/4)\,[(D_{mi})^2 - (D_i)^2]$
Area Moment of Inertia (I), mm^4		
OD Oxide $(I_{ox})_o$	23.5	$(I_{ox})_o = (\pi/64)\,[(D_o)^4 - (D_{mo})^4]$
Metal (I_m)	187.1	$I_m = (\pi/64)\,[(D_{mo})^4 - (D_{mi})^4]$
ID Oxide $(I_{ox})_i$	12.2	$(I_{ox})_i = (\pi/64)\,[(D_{mi})^4 - (D_i)^4]$
Young's Modulus (E) at 135 °C, MPa		
Oxide (E_{ox})	14.8×10^4	MATPRO [3]
Metal (E_m)	8.65×10^4	MATPRO [3]
Equivalent A (A_{eq}) Relative to Metal, mm^2	19.3	$A_{eq} = A_m + (E_{ox}/E_m)\,A_{ox}$
Equivalent I (I_{eq}) Relative to Metal, mm^4	248	$I_{eq} = I_m + (E_{ox}/E_m)\,I_{ox}$
Maximum Bending Moment (M_{max}), N•m	5.7	Measured

For the 4-PBT sample, the maximum tensile stress (σ_{max}) in the metal is related to the maximum bending moment (M_{max}) according to the following:

$$\sigma_{max} = M_{max}\,R_{mo}/I_{eq} \tag{3}$$

where the outer radius ($R_{mo} = D_{mo}/2$) of the metal wall is 5.285 mm.

The maximum tensile stress in the metal is σ_{max} = 5.7 newton meters (N•m) (1,000 millimeters per meter (mm/m)) (5.285 mm)/248 mm^4 = 121.5 megapascals (MPa).

For the axial tensile test, the maximum load (P_{max}) is related to the maximum metal stress (σ_{max}) according to the following:

$$P_{max} = \sigma_{max}\,A_{eq} \tag{4}$$

Setting σ_{max} = 121.5 MPa and A_{eq} = 19.3 mm^2 gives P_{max} = 2,345 N. If the correlation value of 6.3 N•m had been used, then P_{max} = 2,600 N.

The parameters in Table were modified to allow calculations for 18 percent, 20 percent, and 22 percent CP-ECR. The corresponding maximum axial loads to induce failure during fully restrained quench were calculated to be 2,155 N at 18 percent, 1,284 N at 20 percent, and 360 N at 22 percent.

Based on the results for the JAEA fully restrained samples (Refs. 16, 18), the maximum load measured for samples that survived quench from 700 degrees C to less than 100 degrees C was in the range of 1,200 N to 2,400 N. For samples oxidized at 1,200 degrees C to greater than 12 percent BJ-ECR (the equivalent cladding reacted as calculated by the Baker-Just correlation), the maximum was 1,200 to 2,000 N. These results are for cladding with prehydride levels greater than or equal to 100 wppm. Thus, even under these conditions, it appears that the ANL sample from Test OCZL#19 would have survived JAEA fully restrained quench without failure. As the ANL bend tests were performed at 135 degrees C, it would be more proper to say that the 17 percent CP-ECR OCZL#19 sample would have survived the JAEA full-constraint test with quench from 700 degrees C to 135 degrees C.

A similar analysis was performed for the OCZL#12 sample, which had 14 percent maximum CP-ECR in the rupture node and 8 percent ECR at the severed location 40 mm below the rupture midspan. The failure bending moment was 10.5 N•m, and the equivalent cross-sectional area and area moment of inertia were 17.9 mm^2 and 249 mm^4, respectively. Using these values, along with a metal outer radius of 5.467 mm, gives an equivalent axial failure load of 4,127 N, which is much higher than any load measured in the JAEA fully constrained tests.

Equations 3 and 4 can be combined to give the JAEA tensile failure load (P_{max}) as a function of the ANL failure bending moment (M_{max}):

$$P_{max} = M_{max} R_{mo} (A_{eq}/I_{eq})$$

(5)

In principle, Equation 5 can be used for samples that severed in the rupture node (e.g., OCZL#29 at 17 percent CP-ECR). However, the severed cross section for the OCZL#29 sample (49 percent rupture strain) would be similar to the one shown in Figure 7c for the OCZL#18 sample (43 percent rupture strain). The equivalent area and area moment of inertia would have to be calculated numerically for this case. Although the maximum bending moment for the OCZL#29 sample (4.7 N•m) was less than for the OCZL#19 sample (5.7 N•m), the sample did exhibit plastic flow following the first significant load drop and did not sever into two pieces. This adds additional complexity to the determination of the axial load needed to sever the sample at this location.

NRC FORM 335

(12-2010)

NRCMD 3.7

U.S. NUCLEAR REGULATORY COMMISSION

BIBLIOGRAPHIC DATA SHEET

(See instructions on the reverse)

1. REPORT NUMBER
(Assigned by NRC, Add Vol., Supp., Rev.,
and Addendum Numbers, if any.)

NUREG-2119

UNITED STATES
NUCLEAR REGULATORY COMMISSION
WASHINGTON, DC 20555-0001

—————

OFFICIAL BUSINESS

NUREG-2119

Mechanical Behavior of Ballooned and Ruptured Cladding

February 2012